THE
CAMPING
COOKBOOK

HarperCollins*Publishers*
1 London Bridge Street
London SE1 9GF

HarperCollins*Publishers*
1st Floor, Watermarque Building, Ringsend Road
Dublin 4, Ireland

www.harpercollins.co.uk

First published by HarperCollins*Publishers* 2021

10 9 8 7 6 5 4 3 2 1

Food styling by Becks Wilkinson
BBQ and wood-fire cooking by Martin Keane
Props by Jo Harris/Topham Street

A catalogue record of this book is available from the British Library.

HB ISBN 978-0-00-846730-2

Printed and bound in Latvia

When using kitchen appliances, please always follow the manufacturer's instructions.

MIX
Paper from
responsible sources
FSC™ C007454

FSC
www.fsc.org

This book is produced from independently certified FSC™ paper
to ensure responsible forest management.

For more information visit: www.harpercollins.co.uk/green

HEATHER THOMAS

THE
CAMPING
COOKBOOK

Over 60 Delicious Recipes for Every Outdoor Occasion

HarperCollins*Publishers*

CONTENTS

INTRODUCTION

INTRODUCTION

For more and more of us, nothing beats getting back to basics, sleeping in a tent and cooking on a barbecue, a fire pit or a campfire. Food tastes so much better when it's cooked *en plein air* and eaten *al fresco* in the glow of the setting sun. Whether you want to stay on an organised campsite, go upmarket glamping or 'wild' off the grid, you can rustle up quick and easy fabulous meals, whatever the weather, with this handy cookbook.

When you're camping the last thing you want to do is to spend hours slaving over a hot camping stove (or fire) cooking, but savouring the great outdoors gives you an appetite for healthy, filling food. In the following pages, you'll find a selection of simple recipes for breakfasts, snacks and moonlit suppers, as well as sundowner cocktails. By taking the hard work out of campfire cookery, you can effortlessly throw together a tasty meal under the stars with minimal fuss.

The key to success is to use the best-quality fresh ingredients and convenience foods and to cook them in the simplest way. Our delicious recipes are easy to prepare and cook, and most use only a few star ingredients to help streamline your food storage in a small space and make your life simpler. And prepping is quicker when there's less food to chop and grate.

They say that food is good for the soul, and so are a few nights eating out under the stars, and this book shows you how. Everything tastes so much better when it's cooked over hot coals or on an open fire. If you want to get back to nature and enjoy a simpler life, all you need is the right kit, a sense of adventure and this essential cookbook.

GETTING STARTED

Here's some useful information, guidelines and tips to get you started and make your campfire cooking safer and more enjoyable.

COOKING ON A CAMPFIRE

This is traditionally made with wood but some campsites don't permit wood fires and you may have to use charcoal briquettes instead.

1. Choose a site for your fire (see Essential safety rules page 17). If there are no rocky or gravelly areas, dig out a section of turf and place some rocks around the edge – these will be the perimeter of your fire. Ideally, you should light your fire at least an hour before you plan to cook.

2. Collect some dry twigs for kindling wood and place in the centre with some crumpled-up newspaper and firelighters. Cover with some more kindling wood and use matches to set it alight. To speed up this process, you can cheat and use some charcoal briquettes.

3. When the kindling is burning, place some larger logs on top (you can use kiln-dried logs sold in petrol stations). Keep some more logs close by for adding to the fire as the evening goes on.

4. Wait for the flames to die down before you start cooking. If you're planning on ember roasting, you may find it helpful to scrape some hot embers out of the main fire and create a designated and accessible cooking area near the edge. Level them out to fit the size of your pot. When the wood has burnt down to glowing embers, which are grey and ashy, you can place a cast iron pot or skillet directly on top of them. Or you can add corn-on-the-cobs and baking potatoes, wrapped in double-thickness kitchen foil.

5. However, if the embers are still glowing red, raise the pan above the fire – about 10cm (4in) – on a trivet or grill grate, supported on bricks, or suspend it from a camping tripod.

COOKING ON A FIRE PIT

Many campers are turning to portable fire pits as traditional wood fires are not permitted on many campsites and there are often fire restrictions in the wild. A fire pit is safer, easier to control and provides heat and light as well as being a great place to gather and cook. Unless you have a portable propane fire pit, the best fuels to use are kiln-dried logs or wood briquettes. Most fire pits come with a grill grate or rack that fits on top for grilling over the fire. Or you can place a cast-iron pan or frying pan (skillet) directly on the grate. For stews, soups and casseroles, you can hang a saucepan from a tripod above the fire.

COOKING ON A BARBECUE

You can cook on a portable barbecue in the same way as you would at home. Set it up well away from any overhanging trees, bushes or wooden fences. For the best results use sustainably produced charcoal, which is free from fire accelerants. It is not only environmentally friendly but it will also smell nicer and won't affect the taste of the food.

1. Stack the charcoal briquettes or coals on the barbecue with some scrunched-up newspaper and firelighters (use natural ones if possible).

2. Light them and wait for the coals to catch alight and for the flames to die down before cooking over the glowing ashen embers. If there are still flames, wait a little longer.

3. For cooking steaks, chops, burgers and vegetables directly over a high heat, spread out the coals evenly in a single layer. If the coals are glowing white but still a little red in the middle, they are really hot and perfect for direct cooking these types of food.

4. For cooking food slowly (e.g. fish fillets and chicken joints on the bone) or keeping it warm after it has been cooked, push some coals away from one side of the barbecue and place the food on the rack above this area, while more food is cooking directly above the heat on the other side. Or if the coals are very hot but ashen white, you can cook food more slowly above them or place foil parcels within them.

COOKING ON A CAMPING STOVE

Camping has moved on from the primitive one-ring Primus stoves of the past and you can now buy cheap camping stoves with 2-ring burners and a grill. Like a normal hob, you can regulate the amount of heat and use it for boiling water, heating food and cooking in pans and frying pans (skillets). Choose one that is compact, lightweight, portable and can be used in blustery conditions.

 ESSENTIAL SAFETY RULES

Around 90 percent of wildfires are caused by people, including campers, especially when they are staying off-grid, so we all need to follow some basic safety rules.

☑ Don't ignore local fire bans and restrictions.

☑ If fires are not allowed, use a portable fire pit – propane ones are good because they are raised off the ground and you can turn off the fuel source before going to bed.

☑ Never leave a campfire unattended, or to burn overnight – douse it with water to put out the flames.

☑ Don't build a campfire on a grassy spot close to your tent or near brush, shrubs and trees. Choose a gravel or rocky area.

☑ Always wear heatproof gloves and use long-handled tongs with insulated handles when cooking on the fire or a barbecue.

☑ Always keep a bucket of water or a fire extinguisher handy in case you need to put the fire out.

MUST-HAVE EQUIPMENT & GADGETS

You will need some basic portable equipment and handy gadgets for cooking al fresco. We suggest you invest in the following items:

1. A large cast-iron saucepan and a large cast-iron frying pan (skillet). Cast iron is the best material for heat retention and produces an even heat if you place it directly on the fire.

2. A camping kettle.

3. A Dutch oven: a cast-iron covered pot, sometimes with 'legs' to stand in the embers of a campfire, for one-pot meals. You can place glowing embers on the lid to cook food from above and below as in an oven. Use it to sauté, fry, steam, boil, stew or bake.

4. Utensils: a ladle, slotted spoon, wooden spoons, spatula, grater, long metal or wooden skewers, kitchen shears, bottle and tin openers, long-handled BBQ tongs, pan scraper.

5. A water jug and thermos flask.

6. A chopping board and knife, plus a Swiss Army knife.

7. A cool box, camping cooler or portable fridge.

8. A hot pad or trivet to protect tables.

9. Reusable plates and cups to cut down on waste and trash.

10. Lightweight sealable food containers.

11. Camping firelighters: use wind- and waterproof-ones.

12. Matches.

13. Fuel for the fire, fire pit, barbecue or stove: charcoal briquettes or wood, butane, pressurised butane or propane canisters, etc.

14. Bricks and a grill grate for cooking over an open fire.

15. A large roll of kitchen foil for wrapping food on the grill or over the fire.

CAMPING COOKERY TIPS

Cooking in the great outdoors is not like preparing meals in your kitchen at home. But with a little organisation, careful planning and the right equipment, you can still eat like a king.

1. Keep it simple – now is not the time to be adventurous or experimental.

2. Prep ahead and get everyone involved – give them all jobs to do.

3. Limit the number of ingredients to make storage easier and cooking much simpler.

4. Plan your meals and keep all the utensils you need handy.

5. Cover pots and pans when cooking outdoors.

6. Bring pre-measured/weighed and prepped ingredients in ziplock bags or sealed containers, e.g. grated cheese, nuts, seed and spice mixes, vinaigrette, etc.

7. Plan breakfast the night before.

SAFE FOOD STORAGE

It's important to keep food dry, fresh and cool, so it's safe to eat. Always store packaged and fresh foods in airtight sealed containers to protect them from insects and rodents. If you have a portable fridge or camping cooler, use it for chilled and short-life foods. Bottles, jars and tins should be kept in a cool place.

CAMPING CHEATS

Prepare, shop and pack ahead for your trip with healthy convenience foods that don't need refrigeration (or at least until opened), including the following:

1. Tinned beans, lentils and pulses, not dried or fresh.

2. Bottled lemon and lime juice.

3. Tinned vegetables, e.g. tomatoes, mushrooms, artichokes, asparagus, etc.

4. Long-life milk, nut and soya milks, not fresh cow's milk.

5. Easy-cook grains (just soak in water), e.g. couscous, bulgur wheat, quinoa.

6. Tinned salmon, tuna and sardines.

7. Make marinades, sauces, sprinkles in advance or buy ready-made ones.

8. Use ready-made cocktail mixes.

9. Use olive and vegetable oils for cooking, not butter.

10. Use dried herbs rather than fresh if they're not available.

1

BARE NECESSITIES

CAMPING MARINADES

CHILLI CITRUS MARINADE

MAKES 75ML (2½FL OZ/GENEROUS ¼ CUP) | PREP 5 MINUTES

3 tbsp olive oil
juice of 1 small lemon
a good pinch of crushed dried
  chilli flakes

This is so easy to make and great for grilled chicken and prawns (shrimp). For a non-spicy variation, omit the chilli and use some dried or chopped fresh mint, thyme or rosemary instead. Or add crushed garlic or garlic powder.

Put all the ingredients in a sealed plastic container or ziplock bag and shake well. Add the food to be marinated and leave for at least 1 hour before cooking over the fire.

SATAY MARINADE

MAKES 120ML (4FL OZ/½ CUP) | PREP 5 MINUTES

60g (2oz/¼ cup) smooth or
  crunchy peanut butter
3 tbsp olive oil
a good pinch of crushed dried
  chilli flakes
2 tbsp natural low-fat
  yoghurt or coconut cream/
  milk

This quick spicy marinade is perfect for chicken and pork. If you like garlic, add some garlic powder, purée or crushed fresh cloves to taste.

Stir all the ingredients together until well blended and smooth. If it's too thick, slacken with some more yoghurt or coconut cream/milk. Add the meat and leave for at least 1 hour before cooking over the fire.

SRIRACHA MARINADE

MAKES 90ML (3FL OZ/⅓ CUP) | PREP 5 MINUTES

4 tbsp sriracha or other hot
 sauce
1 tbsp sugar
juice of 2 limes or 1 lemon
1 tsp grated fresh root ginger
 or a good squeeze of ginger
 purée (paste)

If you like Asian flavours, this works really well with salmon or chicken. Or substitute soy sauce for the sriracha and use to marinate steak.

Put all the ingredients in a sealed plastic container or ziplock bag and shake well. Add the fish or chicken and leave for 1 hour before cooking over the fire.

HONEY MUSTARD MARINADE

MAKES 90ML (3FL OZ/⅓ CUP) | PREP 5 MINUTES

3 tbsp wholegrain mustard
2 tbsp olive oil
1 tbsp runny honey
1 tsp white wine vinegar
juice of 1 small lemon

Use this for vegetables and tofu as well as steaks and chicken. Vegans can use maple or agave syrup instead of honey. Add some chopped herbs, if wished.

Put all the ingredients in a sealed plastic container or ziplock bag and shake well. Add the food to be marinated and leave for 1 hour before cooking over the fire.

QUICK & EASY BBQ SAUCE

MAKES 400ML (14FL OZ/GENEROUS 1½ CUPS) | PREP 5 MINUTES | COOK 5 MINUTES

300ml (½ pint/1¼ cups) tomato ketchup

2 tbsp Worcestershire sauce

1 tbsp soy sauce

1 tbsp red wine vinegar

1 tbsp Dijon or wholegrain mustard

juice of ½ lemon

2–3 tbsp light brown sugar

½ tsp garlic powder

½ tsp chilli powder or smoked paprika

Tip:
Leave the sauce to cool and use for marinating chicken and spare ribs. Alternatively, serve as a dip for grilled vegetables, prawns (shrimp) and chicken.

You can make this sauce in advance and take it with you in a bottle or sealed plastic container, or you can rustle it up in less than 10 minutes from a few store-cupboard ingredients.

1. Put all the ingredients in a pan and stir well.
2. Set over a medium heat and when the sauce starts to bubble gently, give it a stir and simmer for 4–5 minutes.

Variations
• Use honey instead of brown sugar.
• For a more intense tomato flavour, add 2 tablespoons tomato purée (paste).
• If you don't have a fresh lemon, use bottled concentrated lemon juice to taste.
• Add some heat with a few drops of Tabasco or sriracha.

SEASONINGS & RUBS

You can make these dry seasonings in advance and use them to rub into meat, chicken and fish before grilling or cooking over a fire. For extra flavour, try sprinkling lightly over the cooked food afterwards.

JERK
PREP 5 MINUTES

1 tbsp brown sugar
3 tsp dried thyme
2 tsp ground allspice
1 tsp freshly ground black
  pepper
1 tsp sea salt
1 tsp cayenne pepper
½ tsp ground cinnamon
½ tsp ground nutmeg
½ tsp garlic powder

Use this spicy mixture as a rub for chicken, steak, pork and prawns, or try adding some lime juice, soy sauce and ginger purée (paste) for a wet marinade. For a hotter version, add some chilli powder or deseeded and diced fiery Scotch bonnet chillies.

Mix all the ingredients together and store in an airtight container or screwtop jar.

MIDDLE-EASTERN SEASONING

PREP 5 MINUTES

1 tsp coriander seeds
1 tsp cumin seeds
1 tsp ground cinnamon
1 tsp paprika
½ tsp ground turmeric
½ tsp ground ginger
1 tbsp olive oil

You can make this at home in advance of your camping trip. Use it as a rub for chicken, meat or fish before grilling.

Grind the seeds in a pestle and mortar, then mix in a bowl with the ground spices and olive oil. Transfer to a sealed container.

GREEK LEMON & THYME SEASONING

PREP 5 MINUTES

1 tsp black peppercorns
2 tsp sea salt crystals
1 tbsp chopped thyme leaves
½ tsp garlic powder
grated zest of 2 unwaxed
   lemons

Use this seasoning as a rub for lamb or pork chops and steaks, chicken and fish before grilling. Or mix with olive oil and lemon juice to make a zingy marinade. If wished, use crushed fresh garlic and add some chopped rosemary.

Crush the peppercorns and salt in a pestle and mortar. Mix with the thyme, garlic powder and lemon zest. Store in an airtight container or screwtop jar.

SPRINKLES

You can prepare these sprinkles in advance to take with you in a sealed container or screwtop jar on your camping trip. They keep well for at least one month.

DUKKAH

PREP 5 MINUTES | COOK 4–6 MINUTES

30g (1oz/scant ¼ cup) skinned whole almonds
30g (1oz/¼ cup) shelled pistachios
1 tbsp cumin seeds
1 tbsp coriander seeds
1 tbsp fennel seeds
1 tbsp sesame seeds
a good pinch of fine sea salt

You can sprinkle this Egyptian spiced nutty mixture on halloumi, scrambled eggs, dips, grilled vegetables, white fish and chicken. Vary the nuts and seeds: try adding pine nuts, hazelnuts, pumpkin and sunflower seeds.

1. Toast the nuts in a small dry frying pan (skillet) set over a low to medium heat for 2–3 minutes, shaking the pan occasionally, until lightly golden and fragrant. Remove immediately, taking care that they do not burn. Toast the seeds in the same way.
2. When cool, coarsely grind the nuts and seeds in a pestle and mortar (or pulse briefly in a food processor) – do not overdo it or you'll end up with a powder. Mix with the salt and store in an airtight container or screwtop jar.

CAMPFIRE HERB SPRINKLE

PREP 5 MINUTES

3 tbsp mixed dried herbs,
   e.g. parsley, thyme, basil,
   oregano, marjoram
2 tsp fennel seeds
1 tsp garlic powder
a pinch of fine sea salt
grated zest of 1 unwaxed
   lemon

Sprinkle this herby mixture over cooked chicken, pork, lamb, fish, tofu, halloumi or vegetables, or use as a rub before cooking.

Mix all the ingredients together and store in an airtight container or screwtop jar.

SPICY ZA'ATAR SPRINKLE

PREP 5 MINUTES | COOK 2–3 MINUTES

2 tbsp sesame seeds
2 tbsp sumac
1 tbsp dried marjoram
   or oregano
1 tbsp dried thyme
2 tsp ground cumin
a good pinch of fine sea salt

This goes really well with grilled vegetables, tofu and halloumi, as well as steak and chicken. Scatter it over some goat's cheese, hummus or Baba Ghanoush (see page 118) or mix with some fruity olive oil and use for dipping bread.

1. Toast the sesame seeds in a small dry frying pan (skillet) set over a low to medium heat for 2–3 minutes, shaking the pan occasionally, until lightly golden and fragrant. Remove immediately, taking care that they do not burn.
2. When cool, mix with the other ingredients and store in a sealed container or screwtop jar.

QUICK & EASY SALAD DRESSINGS

SPEEDY SHAKE DRESSING

MAKES APPROX. 90ML (3FL OZ/⅓ CUP) | PREP 5 MINUTES

3 tbsp fruity green olive oil

2 tbsp wine or sherry vinegar

1 red chilli, deseeded and
  diced

a handful of mint, chopped

a pinch of sugar

a pinch of fine sea salt

To keep preparation and chopping to a minimum, you can use some crushed dried chilli flakes instead of fresh chilli. Use this not only on crisp and crunchy salads but also on chargrilled vegetables.

Put all the ingredients in a sealed container or a jam jar with a screwtop lid and shake vigorously until well blended.

ASIAN SESAME DRESSING

MAKES APPROX. 60ML (2FL OZ/¼ CUP) | PREP 5 MINUTES

1 tbsp sesame oil

1 tbsp light olive oil

1 tbsp tamari

juice of 1 small lemon or lime

1 red chilli, deseeded and
  diced (or a pinch of crushed
  dried chilli flakes)

1 tsp runny honey or agave
  syrup

This is great for tossing through crunchy Asian salads, noodles and griddled vegetables. If you don't have tamari use a dark soy sauce instead, although it won't be so thick and intensely flavoured.

Put all the ingredients in a sealed container or a jam jar with a screwtop lid and shake vigorously until well blended.

**Tip:
If you don't have fresh lemons or limes, substitute some bottled juice.**

PEANUT BUTTER DRESSING

MAKES APPROX. 120ML (4FL OZ/½ CUP) | PREP 5 MINUTES

60g (2oz/¼ cup) smooth
   peanut butter
2 tbsp groundnut (peanut)
   or vegetable oil
juice of 1 lime (fresh or
   bottled)
1 tbsp nam pla (Thai fish
   sauce)
1 tbsp rice vinegar
1 tbsp soft brown sugar
a squeeze of garlic purée
   (paste)
a squeeze of ginger purée
   (paste)

You can make this dressing in advance – it will keep well for 4–5 days in a cool place. Use for tossing through crunchy salads or drizzle over grilled chicken, prawns (shrimp) or vegetables.

Blitz all the ingredients in a blender until smooth. Transfer to a sealed container or a jam jar with a screwtop lid.

2

SNACKS

GUACAMOLE

SERVES 4 | PREP 10 MINUTES

½ red onion, diced

1 hot green or red chilli, e.g.
   Scotch bonnet, diced

2 garlic cloves

½ tsp coarse sea salt crystals

2 ripe avocados

juice of 1 lime

a small bunch of coriander
   (cilantro), chopped

1 ripe tomato, deseeded and
   diced

freshly ground black pepper

Tip:
This will keep for 2–3 hours before the avocado starts to discolour.

This is the real thing – freshly made guacamole tastes so much better than ready-made alternatives in jars or from the chilled cabinets in supermarkets. Enjoy as a dip with tortilla chips, potato crisps (chips) or crunchy vegetables. Or serve it with tacos, burritos, fajitas or plain grilled chicken, prawns (shrimp) or vegetables. It's so versatile.

1. Crush the red onion, chilli, garlic and salt in a pestle and mortar.
2. Cut the avocados in half and remove the stones. Scoop out the flesh and mash roughly with a fork. Don't overdo it – you don't want it too smooth. Stir in the lime juice.
3. Add the coriander, crushed red onion mixture and diced tomato. Mix everything together, then grind in some black pepper to finish.

Variations
- Use spring onions (scallions) instead of red onion.
- Diced sunblush tomato makes a good substitute for a fresh one.
- Crushed dried chilli flakes or bottled chillies can replace a diced fresh chilli but won't taste quite so good.

CAMPFIRE NACHOS

SERVES 4 | PREP 15 MINUTES | COOK 10–15 MINUTES

vegetable oil spray

300g (10oz) salted corn
tortilla chips

200g (7oz/1½ cups) hot salsa
or Pico de Gallo (see page 46)

200g (7oz/2 cups) grated
Cheddar or Monterey
Jack cheese

400g (14oz) tin black or
kidney beans, rinsed and
drained

a bunch of spring onions
(scallions), chopped

2 jalapeños, deseeded and
sliced (or pickled or tinned)

1 quantity Guacamole (see
opposite) or 1 large avocado,
diced

Tip:
**If you don't have a lid, you
can cover the Dutch oven or
saucepan with kitchen foil.**

**Delicious, spicy, satisfying, nachos are the best comfort
food and taste best of all when you're sitting with friends
in the warm glow of a campfire. For the best results, you'll
need a cast-iron Dutch oven so you can cook, heat and melt
everything in a single pan. Just build up the layers and it's
easy-peasy. If you don't have a really wide pan, just add
more layers.**

1. Take a large Dutch oven or cast-iron saucepan and lightly
   spray or brush the base with oil.
2. Spread half of the tortilla chips over the base and drizzle
   with half of the salsa or Pico de Gallo. Sprinkle with half of
   the cheese, beans, spring onions and jalapeños.
3. Cover with the remaining chips and salsa and then scatter
   the rest of the beans, spring onions and jalapeños over the
   top. Add the guacamole or avocado and cover with the rest
   of the grated cheese.
4. Cover with a tight-fitting lid and cook on a grill set over the
   fire for 10 minutes. Lift off the lid and check if everything is
   really hot and the cheese has melted. If not, cover and leave
   over the heat for a few more minutes. Serve immediately.

Variations
• Instead of salsa, use a jar or tin of Mexican hot tomato sauce.
• Sprinkle with grated mozzarella for a more stringy texture.
• Serve with coriander (cilantro) and some lime wedges
  for squeezing.
• Add some stoned (pitted) black olives or diced tomatoes.

PIZZAS

SERVES 4 | PREP 15 MINUTES | COOK 7–12 MINUTES

4 large pitta breads, naan breads or flatbreads
olive or vegetable oil, for brushing
8 tbsp passata or bottled Napoletana or pizza sauce
100g (3½oz) bottled roasted red and yellow (bell) pepper strips
200g (7oz) mushrooms, sliced
150g (5oz) mozzarella, packed in brine, sliced
sea salt and freshly ground black pepper

Nothing tastes better than a wood-smoked or chargrilled pizza. We've cheated and made ours with pittas, naan or flatbreads instead of the usual dough bases. They make an easy light meal when you're camping out, especially if you eliminate chopping by using tinned and bottled toppings.

1. When the barbecue is really hot or the campfire flames have died down and the ash is grey, lightly brush one side of the pittas, naan or flatbreads with oil and place them, oiled-side down, on the barbecue grill, or a lightly oiled rack or grill grate set over the fire.
2. When they are lightly browned underneath, remove and brush the other side with oil.
3. Spread the passata or sauce over the grilled side, right up to the edges. Scatter the peppers and mushrooms over them and cover with the mozzarella. Season with salt and pepper.
4. Lay the pizzas on the grill or over the fire. Make a loose 'tent' of kitchen foil and place over the top, or cover with the lid of the barbecue.
5. Cook for 5–10 minutes until the cheese melts and is golden brown and bubbly and the pizza bases are cooked underneath. Remove with a slice or spatula and serve immediately.

Variations
• Here are some ideas for alternative toppings: shredded cooked chicken or ham, pepperoni, sliced sausages, bacon, pineapple, sliced courgettes (zucchini), aubergine (eggplant) or cherry tomatoes.
• If you don't have fresh vegetables use tinned or bottled sweetcorn, artichoke hearts or mushrooms.

BBQ GREEK HALLOUMI WRAPS

SERVES 4 | PREP 15 MINUTES | COOK 6–8 MINUTES

250g (9oz) halloumi, thinly
  sliced
2 tbsp fruity green olive oil
juice of ½ lemon (or bottled)
2 ripe tomatoes, sliced or cut
  into chunks
½ small cucumber, cubed
a few lettuce leaves, e.g. Cos or
  Little Gem
16 juicy black olives, stoned
  (pitted)
1 tbsp red wine vinegar
a good pinch of dried oregano
4 large soft tortilla wraps
sea salt and freshly ground
  black pepper

If you don't have a barbecue grill, you can cook the halloumi and warm the wraps over a campfire or fire pit. Just lay a grill grate or grilling basket over the top. To make these wraps more filling, double the quantity of halloumi and enjoy them for supper.

1 Light a barbecue and wait for it to get medium hot and the flames to die down.
2 Marinate the halloumi in 1 tablespoon of the olive oil and the lemon juice.
3 In a bowl, mix together the tomato, cucumber, lettuce and olives. Blend the remaining oil with the vinegar and oregano. Toss the dressing through the salad and season with salt and pepper.
3 Using tongs, place the halloumi on the bars of the barbecue grill and cook for 2–3 minutes each side until it's slightly charred, golden brown and crisp.
4 Briefly warm the wraps on the grill for about 1 minute each side. Divide the salad among them and top with the halloumi. Roll up or fold over to make a parcel and eat immediately.

Variations
• Use flatbreads instead of wraps.
• Use a bottled vinaigrette dressing.
• Add some sliced red or green (bell) pepper, red onion or spring onions (scallions).
• Add a few crushed dried chilli flakes.
• Drizzle with hot sauce, salsa, Pico de Gallo (see page 46), tahini or yoghurt.

PICO DE GALLO

SERVES 4–6 | PREP 5 MINUTES | STAND 15 MINUTES

6 ripe tomatoes, diced
½ red onion, diced
2 hot chillies, e.g. jalapeños,
 diced (or pickled or tinned)
a handful of coriander
 (cilantro), chopped
juice of 1 lime
a good pinch of fine sea salt

This Mexican fresh 'sauce' is so useful when you're grilling. You can use it as a dip for tortilla chips or raw vegetable sticks, smear it on sandwiches and wraps, drizzle it over nachos and tacos, or serve it with kebabs, sausages, steaks, chicken, chops, halloumi or tofu.

Mix everything together and leave for 15 minutes for the flavours to mingle.

Variations
• Add a chopped white onion or some spring onions (scallions).
• If you don't have a lime, a lemon works too but is less authentic.
• Add 1 or 2 crushed garlic cloves or some garlic powder to taste.
• For a sweeter version, use cherry or baby plum tomatoes.
• Add some diced mango, papaya or avocado.

CAMPFIRE CINNAMON BAKED APPLES

SERVES 4 | PREP 10 MINUTES | COOK 10–18 MINUTES

4 large cooking (green) apples,
   e.g. Bramleys or windfalls
4 tbsp butter, softened
4 tsp soft brown sugar
2 tsp ground cinnamon
2 tbsp raisins

Tip:
**To stop the filling coming
out, leave the bases intact
when you core the apples.**

**The easiest snack or dessert ever! These delicious baked
apples are such a treat and cook quickly in the glowing
embers and coals of a campfire or fire pit.**

1. Using an apple corer, remove the core of each apple. If you
   don't have one, use a sharp knife, working inwards from
   both ends and taking care not to split the apples.
2. Blend 2 tablespoons of the butter with the sugar, cinnamon
   and raisins. Pack it into the centre of each apple and smear
   the remaining butter over the top.
3. Wrap each stuffed apple in a double layer of kitchen foil,
   bringing it up into the centre at the top and twisting the
   ends to form a handle. This will make it easier to lift the
   apples out of the fire.
4. Place them upright in the hot embers of the fire, directly on
   the coals, and cook for 10–18 minutes until cooked, fluffy
   and tender. Unwrap and enjoy!

Variations
- Add some chopped walnuts or dried cranberries, or even
  some porridge oats.
- If you don't have cooking apples, use large Granny Smiths,
  which keep their shape better than other dessert apples.
- Serve drizzled with honey, maple syrup, cream or yoghurt.

CARAMELISED FRUIT KEBABS

SERVES 4 | PREP 15 MINUTES | COOK 5–7 MINUTES

1 small pineapple, peeled,
   cored and cut into chunks
1 ripe mango, peeled, stoned
   (pitted) and cut into chunks
2 bananas, peeled and thickly
   sliced
12 large strawberries, hulled
icing sugar (confectioner's
   sugar), for dusting

Tip:
Make sure you lay the
fruit on a clean grill – not
one you use for cooking
burgers, sausages or fish!

You can use almost any firm fruit that will keep its shape when cut into large chunks and threaded onto skewers. Fruit contains natural sugar and sprinkling it with a little sugar before grilling produces an easy and delicious caramelised dessert.

1. If you're cooking this over a campfire, let it burn down to the embers and place a grill grate over them. If you're using a barbecue, heat it to medium-high.
2. Thread the fruit alternately onto four long skewers. If you are using wooden ones, soak them in water for 20 minutes first to prevent them burning.
3. Dust the kebabs on all sides with icing sugar and set aside for the sugar to dissolve. Place them on a lightly oiled rack set over the fire or a barbecue grill.
4. Cook them, turning frequently, for about 5–7 minutes, until they are hot and starting to caramelise and char slightly. Remove and serve immediately.

Variations
• Experiment with large grapes, melon, papaya (pawpaw), kiwi fruit, apricots or peaches.
• Lightly drizzle with maple syrup or honey before grilling.
• Dust with a little ground cinnamon.
• Serve with ready-made chocolate or salted caramel sauce from a squeezy bottle.

CAMPFIRE TOASTED MARSHMALLOWS

SERVES 4–6 | PREP 2 MINUTES | COOK 3–5 MINUTES

400g (7oz) marshmallows

Tips
- **Metal skewers with wooden handles will prevent them getting too hot to hold or touch.**
- **Wait a minute before biting into the marshmallows – they will be really hot inside and could burn you.**

Toasted marshmallows are the campfire classic – the perfect treat or family dessert, especially for children. When they are heated over a fire, the sugar caramelises and gives them their distinctive smoky flavour. Just skewer them or use a toasting fork and enjoy them plain, or, for delicious s'mores, sandwich them between two chocolate digestive biscuits (graham crackers), which you've warmed over the fire until the chocolate coating starts to melt.

1. Thread the marshmallows on to extra-long thin metal skewers (see tip).
2. If you're toasting them over a fire, wait until it has been burning for a while and the wood has turned to glowing coals. Hold them over the fire, turning them slowly so that they toast evenly, until they are light brown or just starting to char. It will take about 3–5 minutes.
3. It you're toasting them on a barbecue, get it really hot and then hold the skewered marshmallows about 1cm (½in) above the hot coals and cook, rotating them slowly, until gooey and golden brown all over.

Variations
- Dip the toasted marshmallows in melted chocolate or caramel or chocolate sauce.
- Sprinkle the dipped marshmallows with chopped toasted nuts.
- If you're making s'mores, use chocolate Oreos instead of digestives.

3

BREAKFAST & BRUNCHES

ONE-PAN FULL ENGLISH

SERVES 4 | PREP 5 MINUTES | COOK 15 MINUTES

oil, for brushing

4 thin chipolata (links)
   sausages

4 slices of bacon

8 whole chestnut mushrooms

4 tomatoes, halved

4 medium free-range eggs

sea salt and freshly ground
   black pepper

tomato ketchup or brown
   sauce, to serve

Tip:
**You can cover the pan with
kitchen foil or a lid at the
end to set the eggs on top.**

**This is a good way to warm you up and start the day in
the great outdoors. To make your life easy, everything
is cooked in the same pan. This works well on a camping
stove or even on a barbecue grill or over a fire.**

1. If you're cooking this over a campfire, let it burn down to
   the embers and place a grill grate over them. If you're using
   a barbecue, heat it to medium.
2. Lightly brush a large cast-iron frying pan (skillet) with oil
   and set over a medium heat on the camping stove or on the
   barbecue grill or a grate set over the fire.
3. When it's hot, add the sausages and cook, turning, for 3–4
   minutes until browned all over. Add the bacon and cook for
   3 minutes, turning once, until crisp and starting to brown.
4. Add the mushrooms and tomatoes and cook for 3–4
   minutes, turning them once, until softened.
5. Make room in the pan for the eggs and break them into the
   spaces around the bacon, sausages and vegetables. Tilt the
   pan to spread them out and cook for 4–5 minutes until set.
6. Season lightly with salt and pepper and divide among
   four plates. Everybody should end up with one egg, one
   sausage, one bacon slice, two mushrooms and a tomato.
   Serve with tomato ketchup or brown sauce.

Variations
• Instead of breaking in whole eggs, beat them in a bowl and
  then pour into the pan around the other ingredients, so you
  end up with a giant full English omelette (omelet).
• You can add black pudding (boudin noir) or chorizo.
• Use tinned mushrooms instead of fresh.

BREAKFAST BURRITOS

SERVES 4 | PREP 10 MINUTES | COOK 10 MINUTES

6 medium free-range eggs
a few sprigs of coriander
  (cilantro), chopped
oil, for brushing
6 spring onions (scallions),
  sliced
1 red chilli, deseeded and
  diced
4 large tortilla wraps
8 tbsp salsa or Pico de Gallo
  (see page 46)
1 ripe avocado, diced
4 heaped tbsp grated Cheddar
  or Monterey Jack cheese
sea salt and freshly ground
  black pepper

For many happy campers breakfast is the most important meal of the day, especially if you're planning on going hiking, cycling, canoeing or other strenuous outdoor activities. These delicious spicy breakfast burritos will keep you going until lunchtime.

1. If you're cooking this over a campfire, let it burn down to the embers and place a grill grate over them.
2. Beat the eggs in a bowl with the coriander and some salt and pepper.
3. Lightly brush a large frying pan (skillet) with oil and set over a low to medium heat on the camping stove or on a rack set over the campfire. If you're cooking over the fire, use a cast-iron frying pan (skillet). Cook the spring onions and chilli, stirring occasionally, for 3 minutes or until softened.
4. Reduce the heat to low and pour the beaten eggs into the pan. Stir gently until they start to scramble and set. Remove from the heat immediately.
5. Meanwhile, warm the tortillas in a hot pan or in some kitchen foil on the grill.
6. Spread the salsa over the warm tortillas, top with avocado and the scrambled eggs. Sprinkle with grated cheese and fold over into parcels or roll up. Eat immediately.

Variations
- Add some fried mushrooms, cherry tomatoes or bacon.
- If you don't have coriander, chopped parsley or chives work well.
- Add some diced ham or crumbled bacon.
- Serve drizzled with hot sauce.

CORNED BEEF HASH WITH EGGS

SERVES 4 | PREP 5 MINUTES | COOK 15 MINUTES

2 tbsp oil

1 onion, finely chopped or grated

3 medium potatoes, cubed or diced

1 x 350g (12oz) tin corned beef

4 medium free-range eggs

sea salt and freshly ground black pepper

You can knock up this satisfying traditional breakfast in minutes with just a few fresh or tinned ingredients. It's so easy and versatile, too – all the family will love it.

1. Heat the oil in a large frying pan (skillet) on the camping stove. If you're cooking over the fire or a barbecue, use a cast-iron frying pan (skillet). Add the onion and fry over a medium heat for 5 minutes until softened.
2. Stir in the potatoes and cook, stirring occasionally, for 5 minutes or until crisp and golden brown.
3. Add the corned beef to the pan, breaking up any lumps, and heat through for 3–4 minutes.
4. Make four hollows in the mixture and break an egg into each one. Cover the pan with a lid or some kitchen foil and cook for 4–5 minutes until the whites are set but the yolks are still runny. Season with salt and pepper and serve immediately.

Variations
• Use drained tinned potatoes instead of fresh.
• Add some chopped fresh or dried herbs to the hash mixture.
• Serve with tomato ketchup or hot sauce.
• Place a tin of baked beans in the glowing embers of the campfire to heat through, and serve alongside the hash.

MEXICAN CHILLI FRIED EGGS WITH AVOCADO MASH

SERVES 4 | PREP 5 MINUTES | COOK 8–10 MINUTES

2 ripe avocados, peeled and
   stoned (pitted)
2 tsp lemon or lime juice
   (fresh or bottled)
4 large corn tortillas
2 tbsp vegetable oil
4 large free-range eggs
a pinch of crushed dried
   chilli flakes
a small bunch of spring onions
   (scallions), thinly sliced
4 tbsp grated Cheddar or
   Monterey Jack cheese
sea salt and freshly ground
   black pepper
hot sauce, for drizzling
   (optional)

Tip:
**You can buy packs of grated
cheese to take with you.
Most will keep well for
several days even if they
are not stored in a fridge.**

**Another quick and easy no-fuss breakfast that you can
rustle up in a pan. Use a non-stick frying pan (skillet) on
a camping stove or a heavy cast-iron one set over the fire
or barbecue grill. To make this more filling, fry some diced
cooked potatoes in the oil until golden and crispy before
cracking in the eggs, and you'll end up with a hash!**

1. If you're cooking this over a campfire, let it burn down to
   the embers and place a grill grate over them. If you're using
   a barbecue, heat it to medium.
2. Mash the avocados coarsely in a bowl and stir in the lemon
   or lime juice and seasoning to taste. Set aside.
3. Heat the tortillas, one or two at a time, in a dry large frying
   pan (skillet) set over a low to medium heat on the camping
   stove or on the barbecue grill or a grate set over the fire for
   1–2 minutes on each side, just long enough to make them
   golden and slightly crisp. Remove from the pan and keep
   warm until needed.
4. Heat the oil in the pan and fry the eggs until the whites are
   set and crisp around the edges but the yolks are still runny.
   Remove and place on top of the warm tortillas.
5. Add the chilli flakes and spring onions to the pan and
   cook for 1 minute, then spoon over the eggs. Season
   with salt and pepper and sprinkle with grated cheese.
   Serve immediately with the avocado mash and some hot
   sauce, if using.

CAMPING PORRIDGE

Porridge is warming, satisfying and because the oats are low GI (glycaemic index), they release energy slowly to keep you going throughout the day. If you have a camping stove you can make it in minutes in the traditional way (see below) but if you're off-grid in the wild, we have a much simpler 'wild' method.

TRADITIONAL PORRIDGE

SERVES 4 | COOK 5 MINUTES

4 x 120ml (4fl oz) tea cups
   porridge oats
4 x 120ml (4fl oz) tea cups
   milk (dairy or dairy-free)
4 x 120ml (4fl oz) tea cups
   water
a pinch of fine sea salt

Tip:
If you don't have a tea cup for measuring, use a large mug instead and use 2 mugs porridge, 2 mugs water and 2 mugs milk.

There's no need to weigh anything: you just need 1 cup of oats to 2 cups liquid per person. You can use all water or a mixture of water and milk (dairy or non-dairy almond, coconut, oat or soya).

1. Measure the oats in a tea cup into a pan. Add the milk and water and a pinch of salt and stir with a wooden spoon.
2. Set over a medium heat on a camping stove and stir occasionally until the porridge starts to thicken. Turn up the heat to high and when it comes to the boil and starts bubbling cook for 1 minute, stirring.
3. Spoon into bowls and add one of the toppings or sweeteners listed below.

Toppings
- Drizzle with maple syrup, agave syrup, golden (corn) syrup or pomegranate molasses.
- Add a spoonful of apricot or strawberry jam.
- Sprinkle with dark brown (molasses) sugar and a little milk.
- Dust with ground cinnamon or cocoa.
- Sprinkle with chopped nuts, coconut flakes, seeds, granola or dried fruit.

Flavourings
- Swirl in some peanut butter.
- To sweeten the porridge, stir in fresh fruit, e.g. blueberries, raspberries, banana, pears, apples, peaches and figs.
- Swirl in some fruit compôte or stewed apples.
- For a savoury porridge, make in the same way and stir in some grated cheese at the end. Top with fried or grilled mushrooms, cherry tomatoes, crispy bacon or sliced sausages.

'WILD' PORRIDGE

SERVES 4 | COOK 3 MINUTES | SOAK 5–8 MINUTES

2 x 120ml (4fl oz) tea cups
   porridge oats
3 x 120ml (4fl oz) tea cups
   water

Tip:
If you like creamy porridge, you can add a spoonful of milk powder to the oats before stirring in the boiling water.

This quick and easy method is perfect if you have limited equipment and are in a hurry. Just boil a kettle or pan of water over the campfire and get on with other things while the porridge soaks.

1. Put the oats in a heatproof bowl.
2. Bring the water to the boil and pour over the oats. Stir and than cover with a plate and set aside for 5–8 minutes, or until the porridge has thickened and the oats have swelled up and absorbed all the liquid.
3. Stir the porridge, divide among four bowls and add one of the toppings or sweeteners listed opposite.

CAMPFIRE SCRAMBLED EGGS

SERVES 4 | PREP 5 MINUTES | COOK 8–10 MINUTES

6 medium free-range eggs
2 tbsp milk or water
1 tsp butter or vegetable oil
sea salt and freshly ground
   black pepper

Flavourings
You can add the following
to the beaten egg mixture
before cooking:

• Dried or chopped fresh
  herbs.
• Crushed dried chilli flakes or
  diced fresh chilli.
• Finely chopped spring
  onions (scallions).
• Diced ham, bacon or
  smoked salmon.
• Grated cheese or cream
  cheese.
• Diced cooked vegetables,
  e.g. tomatoes, mushrooms,
  peppers, spinach.

Scrambled eggs, cooked in a cast-iron frying pan (skillet) over the fire or a portable camping stove, make a quick and nutritious breakfast. And you can flavour or serve them in so many ways – you can even add the leftovers from last night's supper!

1. If you're cooking this over a campfire, let it burn down to the embers and place a grill grate over them.
2. Lightly beat the eggs and milk or water together with a fork in a jug or bowl. Season with salt and pepper. You can add your flavourings (see left) now, if using.
3. Heat the butter or oil (or a mixture of both) in a cast-iron frying pan (skillet) set over a low to medium heat on the camping stove or a grate set over the fire. When it's hot, pour in the eggs and stir gently with a wooden spoon, pulling the cooked edges in towards the centre, until they start to scramble and thicken. They should be set, moist and fluffy but not runny.
4. Remove from the heat and serve immediately.

Note: If you're doing this over a campfire and can't control the heat, just take the pan off the heat for a few seconds every minute. This will stop the eggs cooking too quickly.

ONE-PAN VEGAN BREAKFAST

SERVES 4 | PREP 10 MINUTES | COOK 12–15 MINUTES

2 tbsp olive oil

300g (10oz) mushrooms, sliced

4 large vine tomatoes, halved

400g (14oz) baby spinach
   leaves

a good pinch of garlic powder

400g (14oz) extra-firm or firm
   tofu

1 tsp soy sauce

a handful of parsley or chives,
   chopped (or use dried)

sea salt and freshly ground
   black pepper

hot sauce, e.g. sriracha, for
   drizzling

Variations

• Add some leftover boiled
  potatoes, cut into chunks
  and fried until golden brown
  and crispy.

• Sprinkle with sunflower,
  pumpkin or fennel seeds.

• Use kale instead of spinach,
  or just add a handful
  of rocket (arugula) or
  watercress at the end.

This healthy vegan fry-up with scrambled tofu is a delicious way to start the day. It's all cooked in the same pan to make your life easier and minimise washing up.

1. If you're cooking this over a campfire, let it burn down to the embers and place a grill grate over them. If you're using a barbecue, heat it to medium.

2. Heat 1 tablespoon of the olive oil in a cast-iron frying pan (skillet) over a medium heat on the camping stove or on the barbecue grill or a grate set over the fire. Cook the mushrooms for 3–4 minutes until golden. Add the tomatoes and cook for 3–4 minutes, then stir in the spinach. Cook for 1 minute, then season with salt and pepper.

3. Transfer to a foil or metal container and keep warm – you can place it at the edge of the fire or grid/rack, or just cover with a lid.

4. Wipe inside the pan with some kitchen paper (paper towels) and then add the remaining oil. Set over a medium to high heat and stir in the garlic powder. Crumble in the tofu with your hands, add the soy sauce and stir gently. Cook for 5 minutes, adding a little water or more soy sauce to keep it moist if it's too dry.

5. Divide the cooked vegetables among four bowls and spoon the scrambled tofu over the top. Sprinkle with herbs and drizzle with hot sauce.

SAUSAGE BREAKFAST SANDWICHES

SERVES 4 | PREP 10 MINUTES | COOK 15 MINUTES

4 fat pork sausages

4 large field or portobello
   mushrooms

a little oil or butter

4 English muffins

4 tsp Dijon or honey mustard

4 slices of Cheddar cheese

sea salt and freshly ground
   black pepper

Breakfast tastes even better outside when you eat it with your hands rather than knives and forks. If you're in a hurry to move off or go for a hike, this is the perfect on-the-go sandwich.

1. Grill the sausages in a cast-iron frying pan (skillet) over hot coals on a barbecue or on a rack over the glowing embers of the campfire, turning occasionally, for about 10 minutes or until cooked through and browned all over.
2. After 5 minutes, place the mushrooms on the grill. Drizzle with a little oil or dot with butter and cook for 5 minutes until tender and golden brown.
3. Meanwhile, split the muffins and toast them lightly on the grill.
4. Spread a little mustard on each muffin and fill each one with a sausage, cut in half, and a grilled mushroom. Season with salt and pepper and top with a slice of cheese.
5. Wrap each muffin in a square of kitchen foil, twisting the ends to seal it. Place on the grill or over the fire for about 4–5 minutes or until the cheese melts. Eat immediately.

Variations
• Serve with tomato ketchup or hot sauce.
• Add a fried egg or a slice of beefsteak tomato to each muffin.
• Instead of pork sausages, use vegetarian Quorn ones, or even a slice of grilled halloumi or tofu.
• Add some crushed garlic and/or herbs to the mushrooms while grilling them.

FLASH
IN THE PAN

EASY SUPPERS

FORAGED CAMPFIRE RISOTTO

SERVES 4–6 | PREP 10 MINUTES | COOK 35–40 MINUTES

4 tbsp olive oil

1 large onion, diced

3 garlic cloves, crushed,
   or foraged wild garlic,
   chopped

350g (12oz) mushrooms, sliced
   (wild or cultivated)

400g (14oz/2¼ cups) risotto
   rice

120ml (4fl oz/½ cup) white
   wine

1.2 litres (2 pints/5 cups) hot
   vegetable or chicken stock
   (broth), made with a stock
   cube

a few handfuls of shredded
   greens, e.g. spinach, spring
   greens, sorrel

a handful of herbs, chopped

sea salt and freshly ground
   black pepper

grated cheese, e.g. Parmesan,
   to serve

Tip:
**If you don't have a two-
burner camp stove to keep
the stock hot, make it up
and keep in a large flask.**

**This risotto is a movable feast – you can add almost
anything edible that you can forage in hedgerows, woods
and on the coast. Any wild greens, herbs, garlic, celery,
sorrel, nettles and mushrooms will taste fabulous. This
is best cooked on a camping stove to control the heat and
enable you to stir it safely, but you can set the frying pan
(skillet) on a grill grate over the glowing embers of the fire.**

**CAUTION! If using wild foraged mushrooms, make sure
that they are safe. If you're not certain, do not use them.**

1. Heat the olive oil in a large cast-iron frying pan (skillet) set
   over a low to medium heat on the camping stove. Cook the
   onion and garlic, stirring occasionally, for 8–10 minutes until
   softened. Stir in the mushrooms and cook for 5 minutes or
   so, until golden brown.
2. Add the rice and stir until the grains are glistening. Cook for
   2–3 minutes and then pour in the wine. Let it bubble away
   until it evaporates.
3. Now start adding the stock, a little at a time and stirring
   occasionally. When it's been absorbed by the rice, add some
   more. Keep on doing this for about 20 minutes until all or
   most of the stock has been absorbed and the rice is plump
   and tender but still has some 'bite'.
4. Stir in the greens and herbs and let them wilt into the risotto.
   Check the seasoning, adding salt and pepper if required.
5. Serve in bowls sprinkled with grated Parmesan.

Variations
• If you don't have fresh mushrooms, soak some dried porcini in
   hot water.

SPEEDY CREAMY CHICKEN & MUSHROOMS

SERVES 4 | PREP 10 MINUTES | COOK 25 MINUTES

3 tbsp olive oil

500g (1lb 2oz) chicken breasts, cubed

1 large onion, finely chopped

2 garlic cloves, crushed

400g (14oz) white or chestnut mushrooms, quartered

1 x 400g (14oz) tin cream of mushroom soup

freshly ground black pepper

a handful of parsley, finely chopped

Supper doesn't get easier than this. All you do is sauté some chicken and vegetables in a frying pan (skillet) and then pour in a tin of soup and cook for 10 minutes. You can rustle it up on a camping stove or on a grill over the hot embers of a campfire.

1. If you're cooking this over a campfire, let it burn down to the embers and place a grill grate over them.
2. Heat the oil in a cast-iron frying pan (skillet) over a medium heat on the camping stove or a grate set over the fire. When it's hot, add the chicken and cook briskly, turning them frequently, for about 5 minutes, until golden brown all over.
3. Add the onion, garlic and mushrooms and cook for 8–10 minutes, until the onion has softened and the mushrooms are golden brown.
4. Pour in the soup and simmer gently for 10 minutes. Check the seasoning, adding a grinding of black pepper to taste.
5. Serve immediately, sprinkled with parsley, with some hot noodles, plain boiled rice or potatoes.

Variations
• Add a dash of sherry, wine or vermouth at the end of step 3.
• Stir in some baby spinach leaves, drained artichoke hearts or bottled grilled peppers.
• Add some grated lemon zest and a squeeze of juice.

GREEN SALMON FRITTATA

SERVES 4 | PREP 10 MINUTES | COOK 15–20 MINUTES

1 tbsp olive oil

6 spring onions (scallions),
finely sliced

150g (5oz) watercress or baby
spinach leaves

2 x 200g (7oz) tins wild Pacific
salmon, drained and flaked

a pinch of crushed dried chilli
flakes

8 medium free-range eggs

4 tbsp milk

a good pinch of ground
nutmeg

50g (2oz/½ cup) grated
Cheddar or Swiss cheese

sea salt and freshly ground
black pepper

Tip:
If your pan doesn't have a
lid, you can use the lid from
a Dutch oven or just cover
with kitchen foil.

This frittata is light but fills you up surprisingly well. Eat
it with a salad and crusty bread for supper or serve it
for breakfast. You can even eat it lukewarm or cold for a
packed lunch. To cook the frittata you'll need a cast-iron
frying pan (skillet), preferably with a lid. You can also cook
it on a camping stove.

1. If you're cooking this over a campfire, let it burn down to
   the embers and place a grill grate over them. If you're using
   a barbecue, heat it to medium.
2. Place a large cast-iron frying pan (skillet) over the glowing
   embers of the fire or the barbecue grill. Add the oil and
   when it gets hot, cook the spring onions for 2–3 minutes
   until softened. Add the watercress or spinach and stir until
   it begins to wilt. Stir in the salmon and chilli.
3. In a bowl, beat the eggs with the milk, nutmeg and some
   salt and pepper.
4. Pour the eggs into the pan and stir gently. Sprinkle the cheese
   over the top. Cover with a lid and cook for 10–15 minutes,
   until the frittata is cooked and golden brown underneath and
   the top has set. Check after 10 minutes to make sure it's not
   too brown underneath – raise the grill grate if necessary.
5. Remove from the heat and serve the frittata cut into wedges.

Variations
- Use diced smoked salmon or flaked hot smoked salmon
  instead of tinned.
- Almost any greens work well, including shredded spinach,
  spring greens, sorrel, rocket (arugula) or foraged greens.

PAN-FRIED LEMONY PORK CHOPS

SERVES 4 | PREP 10 MINUTES | COOK 8 MINUTES

4 x 2.5cm (1in) thick pork
   chops
2 tbsp olive oil, plus extra for
   brushing
2 tsp Greek Lemon & Thyme
   Seasoning (see page 31)
sea salt and freshly ground
   black pepper

Lemon dressing

2 tbsp fruity green olive oil
juice of 1 lemon
1 tsp Dijon mustard
1 garlic clove, crushed
a handful of parsley, finely
   chopped

Tip:
**You can add some white
wine and cream to the pan
at the end. Let it bubble
up and reduce to a creamy
sauce with the pan juices
and scrapings.**

**You can use boneless or on-the-bone pork chops to make
this delicious supper dish. It's so easy to prepare and
cooks in minutes for a really fast meal when you're feeling
ravenous after a busy day in the great outdoors.**

1. If you're cooking this over a campfire, let it burn down to
   the embers and place a grill grate over them. If you're using
   a barbecue, heat it to medium.
2. Pat dry the pork chops with some kitchen paper (paper
   towels). Lightly brush both sides with olive oil and season
   with plenty of salt and pepper.
3. Heat the olive oil in a large cast-iron frying pan (skillet) set
   over a medium to high heat on a camping stove or on the
   barbecue grill or a grate set over the fire.
4. Add the chops and cook for about 4 minutes each side, or
   until they are cooked right through and appetisingly brown
   on the outside. Remove from the pan and rest for
   5 minutes.
5. While the chops are cooking, make the lemon dressing: put
   the ingredients in a screw-top jar and give it a good shake.
6. Serve the pork chops with the lemon dressing drizzled over
   the top. Baked potatoes or corn-on-the-cobs and some
   salad make a good accompaniment.

Variations
• You can use any dry rub or seasoning mix (see pages 29–31).
• Serve with some apple sauce or jelly.
• Vary the dressing: try orange juice and grated zest, chopped
coriander (cilantro), thyme or rosemary.
• Cook thick lamb chops in the same way.

74   **FLASH IN THE PAN**

PAN-FRIED SAUSAGES & RED CABBAGE

SERVES 4 | PREP 10 MINUTES | COOK 30 MINUTES

2 tbsp olive oil

8 pork sausages

1 red onion, thinly sliced

½ red cabbage, cored and
   thickly sliced

2 red apples, cored and cut
   into quarters

a pinch each of ground
   cinnamon and nutmeg

240ml (8fl oz/1 cup) cider or
   red wine

1 tbsp cider vinegar or red
   wine vinegar

sea salt and freshly ground
   black pepper

mustard, to serve

You'll need a large cast-iron frying pan (skillet) to cook this simple supper. It really warms you up on a cold night – perfect for eating round a campfire under the stars.

1. If you're cooking this over a campfire, let it burn down to the embers and place a grill grate over them. If you're using a barbecue, heat it to medium.
2. Heat the olive oil in a large cast-iron frying pan (skillet) set over a medium heat on the camping stove or on the barbecue grill or a grate set over the fire. Add the sausages and cook, turning occasionally, for about 5 minutes or until browned all over.
3. Add the onion and cook for 5 minutes or until softened. Gently stir in the red cabbage, apples and spices and cook, stirring occasionally, for 5 minutes.
4. Pour in the cider or wine and the vinegar and reduce the heat or raise the grid or grill grate higher above the fire. Cook gently for 15 minutes or until the sausages are thoroughly cooked, the cabbage is tender and the liquid has evaporated.
5. Season with salt and pepper to taste and serve immediately with mustard and some crusty bread or baked potatoes.

Variations
- You can use chicken stock (broth) instead of cider or wine.
- Use green or white cabbage instead of red.
- Serve sprinkled with chopped herbs or pomegranate seeds.
- Vegetarians can use any meatless or plant-based sausages.

MOZZARELLA MUSHROOM CHICKEN

SERVES 4 | PREP 5 MINUTES | COOK 15 MINUTES

3 tbsp olive oil

4 boneless chicken breasts, skinned

300g (10oz) mushrooms, sliced

250g (9oz) mozzarella, thinly sliced

sea salt and freshly ground black pepper

pesto sauce, for drizzling (optional)

Tip:
This will cook more quickly if you flatten the chicken breasts first with a meat mallet or rolling pin.

One of the easiest campfire suppers of all time! This cooks everything in a cast-iron frying pan (skillet) but you could use a Dutch oven instead or even wrap the chicken, mushrooms and mozzarella in a foil package and cook it over the hot coals of a barbecue or the glowing embers of the campfire.

1. If you're cooking this over a campfire, let it burn down to the embers and place a grill grate over them. If you're using a barbecue, heat it to medium.
2. Heat the olive oil in a large cast-iron frying pan (skillet) set over a medium heat on the camping stove or on the barbecue grill or a grate set over the fire. Add the chicken and cook for 2–3 minutes each side until golden brown.
3. Add the mushrooms and cook gently, stirring occasionally, for 5 minutes or until tender and golden. Season with salt and pepper.
4. Scatter the sliced mozzarella over the chicken and mushrooms and cover the pan with a lid – if you don't have one, use a sheet of kitchen foil. Cook for 5 minutes until the mozzarella melts and the chicken is cooked through.
5. Serve immediately, drizzled with pesto sauce (if using), with some crusty bread to wipe up the delicious cheesy juices.

Variations

- You can use ready-grated mozzarella instead of fresh.
- Sprinkle with chopped herbs, e.g. parsley or basil.
- Add some crushed garlic with the mushrooms.
- Season the chicken with some paprika or garlic powder before cooking.

PIZZA PITTA POCKETS

SERVES 4 | PREP 10 MINUTES | COOK 15 MINUTES

2 tbsp olive oil

1 onion, thinly sliced

3 red, yellow or green (bell) peppers, deseeded and thinly sliced

4 large pitta breads

240ml (8fl oz/1 cup) spaghetti or pizza tomato sauce (ready-made from a jar)

100g (3½oz/1 cup) grated mozzarella

You can make these quick 'pizzas' in a cast-iron frying pan (skillet) on the campfire or above the hot coals on a barbecue. They are infinitely versatile and you can add almost any flavourings (see the variations below). All the family, especially children, will love them.

1. If you're cooking this over a campfire, let it burn down to the embers and place a grill grate over them. If you're using a barbecue, heat it to medium.
2. Heat the olive oil in a large cast-iron frying pan (skillet) set over a medium heat on the barbecue grill or a grate set over the fire. Cook the onion and peppers for 6–8 minutes, until tender and softened.
3. Cut each pitta pocket in half through the middle, so you end up with eight pockets.
4. Spread some tomato sauce inside each pocket (top and bottom) and fill with the fried onion and peppers. Top with the grated cheese.
5. Wrap the pittas individually in kitchen foil and place over the hot coals on the campfire or barbecue. Cook for 2–3 minutes each side, just long enough to warm through and for the cheese to melt.

Variations
- Add some diced cooked chicken, chorizo, peperoni, ham or bacon.
- Add some tinned sweetcorn kernels or pineapple chunks.
- Use drained bottled chargrilled (bell) peppers instead of fresh ones.
- Wrap the filling in a tortilla instead of a pitta bread.

SPICY APPLE PAN CRUMBLE

SERVES 4 | PREP 15 MINUTES | COOK 25–40 MINUTES

4 large cooking (green) apples,
 e.g. Bramleys, peeled, cored
 and cut into wedges
4 tbsp brown sugar, e.g.
 Demerara
¼ tsp ground cinnamon
4 tbsp butter
juice of ½ lemon
4 tbsp apple juice (or water)

Crumble topping

75g (2½oz/⅓ cup) softened
 butter
75g (2½oz/¾ cup) plain
 (all-purpose) flour
50g (2oz/½ cup) porridge oats
50g (2oz/½ cup) chopped nuts,
 e.g. almonds, hazelnuts or
 walnuts
6 tbsp brown sugar, e.g.
 Demerara

Variations

• Add some ground almonds
 (almond meal) to the
 crumble mixture.
• Add some foraged
 blackberries to the apples.

Did you know that you can create some of your favourite desserts in a cast-iron frying pan (skillet) over the campfire? This crumble is the perfect way to finish the day. Serve it with some cream (long-life if you can't get fresh) or some ready-made shop-bought custard. If you don't have a skillet, you can use a Dutch oven instead.

1. If you're cooking this over a campfire, let it burn down to the embers and place a grill grate over them. If you're using a barbecue, heat it to medium.
2. Make the crumble topping: rub the butter into the flour with your fingertips and then stir in the oats, nuts and sugar. Toast the mixture gently in a frying pan until nice and golden, then set aside.
3. Toss the apples in the sugar and cinnamon. Melt the butter in a large frying pan (skillet) over a medium heat on the camping stove or on the barbecue or a grate set over the glowing coals of the fire. If you're cooking over the fire or on the barbecue grill, use a cast-iron frying pan (skillet). Add the apples, lemon juice and apple juice and cook, stirring occasionally, for 5–10 minutes, or until golden and starting to soften.
4. Sprinkle the crumble topping over the apples and cover the pan with a lid. If you don't have one, use a 'tent' of kitchen foil or, if on a covered barbecue, lower the cover.
5. Cook for 20–30 minutes or until the topping is crisp and the apples are bubbling through.

Note: If you don't have cooking apples, use 8 firm dessert apples, such as Granny Smiths.

5

ONE-POT
WONDERS

FISHY TOMATO ONE-POT SPAGHETTI

SERVES 4 | PREP 10 MINUTES | COOK 20 MINUTES

3 tbsp fruity green olive oil

1 onion, diced

2 garlic cloves, crushed

1 x 400g (14oz) tin chopped
   tomatoes

1 x 400g (14oz) jar tomato
   pasta sauce, e.g. Napoletana,
   arrabbiata or basilico

240ml (8fl oz/1 cup) water

4 tbsp capers, rinsed

400g (14oz) thin spaghetti
   (dried weight)

2 x 125g (4½oz) tins sardines
   in olive oil, drained OR 2 x
   145g (5oz) tins tuna in olive
   oil or spring water, drained

sea salt and freshly ground
   black pepper

chopped parsley or torn basil
   or rocket (arugula), to serve

In this easy campfire recipe, the spaghetti cooks in the coating sauce in the cast-iron pot over the hot embers of the fire. Use the best-quality tinned sardines or tuna you can find, so you can add some of the drained fishy olive oil to the pasta sauce. You can also make this in a heavy pot on a camping stove.

1. Heat the oil in a Dutch oven set over the glowing embers of the campfire. Cook the onion and garlic for 6–8 minutes until tender.
2. Add the tomatoes, tomato sauce, water and capers. Stir well and then add the spaghetti. You may have to break the strands in half to fit them in the pan. Cook for 10 minutes, or until the sauce has thickened and the pasta is cooked to the bite (al dente). If the sauce is too thick for your liking, you can add a little water to thin it.
3. Stir in the sardines or tuna, adding a little of the fishy oil from the tin for flavour, if wished. Season with salt and pepper.
4. Serve in bowls, sprinkled with parsley, basil or rocket.

Variations
- Sprinkle with some crisp fried breadcrumbs.
- If you don't have fresh garlic, use some garlic powder.
- Spice up the sauce with some crushed dried chilli flakes.
- Add some aubergine (eggplant) or fennel.
- The Italians would think it heresy to serve cheese with fish but you could scatter some grated Parmesan over the top.

SPEEDY BEEF & BLACK BEAN CHILLI

SERVES 4 | PREP 10 MINUTES | COOK 1¼ HOURS

2 tbsp olive oil

1 large onion, chopped

3 garlic cloves, crushed

1 red (bell) pepper, deseeded
and diced

2 tsp hot chilli powder

½ tsp cayenne

500g (1lb 2oz/generous 2 cups)
minced (ground) beef

2 x 400g (14oz) tins chopped
tomatoes

2 tbsp tomato purée (paste)

1 x 400g (14oz) tin black
beans, rinsed and drained

240ml (8fl oz/1 cup) beef stock
(broth)

100g (3½oz/1 cup) coarsely
grated Cheddar cheese

sea salt and black pepper

tortilla chips, flatbreads, or
crusty bread, to serve

Tip:
If you're cooking this over
the fire, try to keep the
heat even and add more
logs or charcoal briquettes
if necessary.

Make this delicious chilli in a cast-iron Dutch oven over the
fire or on a camping stove. A Dutch oven is such a useful
pan when you're camping because heat is applied to the
food from above as well as below, so it cooks more evenly
and everything can be done in the same pan.

1. If you're cooking this over a campfire, let it burn down to
   the embers and place a grill grate over them.
2. Heat the oil in the Dutch oven or a large cast-iron pot set
   over a medium heat on the camping stove or on a grate set
   over the fire. Cook the onion, garlic and red pepper, stirring
   occasionally, for 8–10 minutes until softened. Stir in the
   spices and cook for 1 minute.
3. Add the minced beef and cook for 5–10 minutes, stirring
   occasionally, until browned all over.
4. Add the tomatoes, tomato paste, tinned beans and stock.
   Cover the pot and simmer for 30 minutes. Remove the lid
   and cook, uncovered, for another 30 minutes, or until the
   liquid has reduced to a fragrant spicy sauce. Season to
   taste with salt and pepper.
5. Serve in bowls, sprinkled with grated cheese, with some
   tortilla chips, warmed flatbreads or pittas, or crusty bread
   for dipping and wiping the bowls.

Variations
• If you don't have any minced beef, just make a vegetarian
  version. Add more onions, peppers and another tin of beans.
• Use red kidney beans instead of black ones.
• Use tinned or bottled jalapeños for a really hot chilli.
• If you don't have fresh garlic, substitute garlic powder.

LENTIL SLOPPY JOES

SERVES 4 | PREP 10 MINUTES | COOK 35 MINUTES

2 tbsp olive oil

1 onion, finely chopped

3 garlic cloves, crushed

5 tbsp tomato purée (paste)

1 x 200g (7oz) jar tomato pasta
 sauce, e.g. Napoletana,
 arrabbiata or basilico

200g (7oz/1 cup) red lentils
 (dried weight)

360ml (12fl oz/1½ cups)
 vegetable stock (broth)
 made with bouillon powder
 or a stock cube

1–2 tbsp coconut sugar or
 maple syrup

1 tsp cider vinegar

1 tsp Dijon mustard

1 tbsp vegan Worcestershire
 sauce

1 tsp chilli powder

4 large burger buns

sea salt and freshly ground
 black peppers

sliced red onion, tomatoes and
 lettuce, to serve (optional)

Sloppy Joes are great camping food – they're easy to make, don't require any specialist ingredients, cook in one pot and, best of all, you can eat them in your hands. This version, made with lentils, is perfect for vegans and vegetarians but they're so tasty that meat lovers will enjoy them, too.

1. Heat the oil in a Dutch oven set over the glowing embers of the campfire. Alternatively, cook in a cast-iron frying pan (skillet) on the barbecue or over medium heat on a camping stove. Cook the onion and garlic for 6–8 minutes until tender.
2. Stir in the tomato purée and pasta sauce, and then add the lentils and stock. Cover and cook for 15 minutes or until the lentils are tender but not mushy and most of the liquid has been absorbed.
3. Stir in the coconut sugar or maple syrup (to taste), vinegar, mustard, Worcestershire sauce and chilli powder. Cook for 10 minutes or until the lentil mixture is thick. Season to taste with salt and pepper.
4. Split and toast the burger buns on a grill over the fire and fill with the lentil mixture. If wished, add some lettuce, red onion or tomato. Eat immediately.

Variations
- Spice these up with some ground cumin or smoked paprika.
- Add some diced red or green (bell) pepper.
- If you like hot spicy food, add more chilli powder or drizzle with hot sauce.

CAMPFIRE RUSTIC BEAN SOUP

SERVES 4 | PREP 15 MINUTES | COOK 50 MINUTES

2 tbsp olive oil

2 onions, chopped

2 large carrots, diced

2 garlic cloves, crushed

900ml (1½ pints/3¾ cups)
vegetable stock (broth)
made with bouillon powder
or a stock cube

1 x 400g (14oz) tin chopped
tomatoes

2 tbsp tomato purée (paste)

½ tsp dried thyme or oregano

2 x 400g (14oz) tins
butterbeans (lima beans),
rinsed and drained

1 small green cabbage,
coarsely shredded or cut
into small wedges

sea salt and freshly ground
black pepper

grated cheese and crusty
bread, to serve

A hearty vegetable and bean soup will warm you up at the end of the day. Let it bubble away in the Dutch oven while you sit in the firelight enjoying a drink and some nibbles. You can also make this soup in a pan on a camping stove.

1. If you're cooking this over a campfire, let it burn down to the embers and place a grill grate over them.
2. Heat the oil in the Dutch oven and set over a medium heat on the camping stove or on a grate set over the fire. Cook the onion, carrot and garlic, stirring occasionally, for about 10 minutes until softened but not coloured.
3. Add the stock, tomatoes, tomato purée and herbs and cover the pan with the lid. Cook for 30–40 minutes, or until all the vegetables are cooked and tender.
4. Stir in the beans and cabbage. Cover and cook for 5 minutes or just long enough for the greens to wilt without losing their texture and colour. Season to taste with salt and pepper.
5. Ladle the soup into bowls and serve immediately, sprinkled with grated cheese, with some crusty bread on the side.

Variations

• Add some celery, leeks, potatoes, courgettes (zucchini) or fennel for an added veggie kick.
• You can use any tinned beans, e.g. borlotti, cannellini, kidney or black beans.
• For a more filling soup, add some small penne or soup pasta 10 minutes or so before the end of cooking.
• Stir in some pesto at the end.

88 **ONE-POT WONDERS**

ONE-POT MAC 'N CHEESE

SERVES 4 | PREP 5 MINUTES | COOK 10–15 MINUTES

300g (10½oz/3 cups) macaroni
(dried weight)
480ml (16fl oz/2 cups) milk
240ml (8fl oz/1 cup) water
2 tbsp butter
240ml (8fl oz/1 cup)
evaporated milk
300g (11oz/3 cups) grated
cheese, e.g. Swiss, Cheddar,
Parmesan
1 tbsp Dijon mustard
a good pinch of garlic powder
sea salt and freshly ground
black pepper
cayenne or chilli powder, for
dusting

Tip:
You can just cook the pasta as directed above and then stir in a jar of store-bought cheese or alfredo sauce.

You will need a Dutch oven or a covered heavy cast-iron saucepan to cook this delicious supper as it applies heat from the top as well as the bottom … rather like a conventional oven. The result is that the pasta steams inside the pan and cooks to perfection.

1. If you're cooking this over a campfire, let it burn down to the embers and place a grill grate over them.
2. Put the macaroni, milk, water, butter and a good pinch of salt in a large Dutch oven. Cover with the lid.
3. Place over the fire and put some glowing hot coals on the lid. Cook for 10 minutes, or until the macaroni is just tender but retains some 'bite' and there's still a little cooking liquid in the pan.
4. Raise the Dutch oven higher up above the fire on a tripod or grid and stir in the evaporated milk, cheese, mustard and garlic powder. Keep stirring until the cheese melts and the sauce coats the pasta.
5. Season to taste with salt and pepper and serve immediately, dusted lightly with cayenne or chilli powder.

Variations
• Stir in some baby spinach leaves, diced spring onions (scallions), cherry tomatoes or a diced jalapeño chilli at the end.
• Add some diced ham or crispy bacon bits.
• Use a mixture of crumbled blue cheese and grated cheese.
• Sprinkle with chopped parsley or chives.
• For a crunchy topping, sprinkle with crushed cheesy crackers, potato crisps (chips) or tortilla chips.

QUICK SAUSAGE & BEANS CASSEROLE

SERVES 4 | PREP 10 MINUTES | COOK 25 MINUTES

1 tbsp olive oil

8 pork sausages

1 large onion, diced

3 garlic cloves, crushed

1 chilli, diced

1 x 400g (14oz) tin baked beans

1 x 400g (14oz) tin cannellini, kidney or black beans, rinsed and drained

1 x 400g (14oz) tin chopped tomatoes

a dash of Worcestershire sauce (optional)

sea salt and freshly ground black pepper

crusty bread or flatbreads, to serve

This cowboy-style supper is really simple to throw together and best eaten in the flickering light of a campfire under the stars. Vegetarians and vegans can substitute any meat-free sausages.

1. Place a Dutch oven or large cast-iron frying pan (skillet) on a tripod or grill grate over the glowing embers of the campfire when the flames have died down. When it's hot, add the oil and cook the sausages, turning them occasionally, for about 5 minutes until they are browned all over.

2. Add the onion, garlic and chilli and cook for 6–8 minutes until softened.

3. Stir in both tins of beans, the tomatoes and Worcestershire sauce (if using) and cook for 10 minutes, or until everything is cooked and the liquid has reduced and thickened. Check the seasoning before adding any salt. It will probably need pepper but there's quite a lot of salt in most tins of beans.

4. Serve in bowls with crusty bread or flatbreads to mop up the sauce.

Variations
• If you don't have a fresh chilli, use 1–2 tsp chilli powder.
• Use garlic powder instead of fresh.
• Serve it with rice, quinoa or boiled pasta.
• Add some diced bacon or crispy grilled slices.
• Add some diced red (bell) pepper or carrots.
• For a really rich tomato sauce, add some tomato purée (paste).

CHICKEN CHORIZO COUSCOUS

SERVES 4 | PREP 10 MINUTES | COOK 30–35 MINUTES | STAND 10 MINUTES

1 chorizo sausage, sliced

8 boneless chicken thighs, cut in half

1 large onion, diced

3 garlic cloves, crushed

2 red (bell) peppers, deseeded and cut into chunks

1 tsp chilli powder

2 tsp smoked paprika

400ml (14fl oz/generous 1½ cups) chicken stock (broth) made with bouillon powder or a stock cube

1 x 400g (14oz) tin chickpeas, rinsed and drained

1 x 400g (14oz) tin chopped tomatoes

175g (6oz/1 cup) couscous (dried weight)

hummus or harissa, to serve

Note:
You won't need to add olive oil because a lot of fat comes out of the chorizo as it cooks.

For the best flavour, cook this spicy couscous in a cast-iron saucepan or Dutch oven set over an open fire, but it also works well in a deep cast-iron frying pan (skillet) on a barbecue or camping stove. It's so easy to make and very filling at the end of a busy day in the great outdoors.

1. If you're cooking this over a campfire, let it burn down to the embers and place a grill grate over them. If you're using a barbecue, heat it to medium.

2. Heat the Dutch oven or frying pan (skillet) over the campfire or on the barbecue or camping stove.

3. When it's hot, add the chorizo and chicken and cook, stirring occasionally, for about 6–8 minutes, or until the red oil runs out of the chorizo and the chicken is browned all over.

4. Add the onion, garlic and peppers and cook, stirring, for 5 minutes, or until softened. Stir in the chilli powder and smoked paprika and cook for 1 minute.

5. Add the stock, chickpeas and tomatoes and cook for 15–20 minutes until the vegetables and chicken are cooked.

6. Stir in the couscous and remove the pan from the heat. Cover with the lid or some kitchen foil and leave it to stand for 10–15 minutes, or until the couscous swells up and most of the liquid is absorbed. Fork it though gently to separate any clumps and serve immediately with some hummus or fiery harissa paste.

Variations
- Add some vegetables, e.g. peas, aubergine (eggplant) or courgettes (zucchini).
- Serve with some yoghurt or Baba Ghanoush (see page 118) or sprinkle with pomegranate seeds.

92

CHEAT'S CAMPFIRE FRUITY COBBLER

SERVES 4 | PREP 10 MINUTES | COOK 35–45 MINUTES

300g (10oz/3 cups) mixed
  berries, e.g. strawberries,
  blueberries, raspberries
4 peaches or nectarines,
  stoned (pitted) and cut
  into chunks
50g (2oz/¼ cup) sugar, plus
  extra for sprinkling
1 tsp ground cinnamon
4 tsp cornflour (cornstarch)
1–2 tbsp butter

Cobbler topping
115g (4oz/1 cup) plain (all-
  purpose) flour
1 tsp baking powder
3 tbsp Demerara sugar
a pinch of salt
4 tbsp butter, softened, plus
  extra for greasing
4 tbsp milk

Tip:
**Place the Dutch oven on
a grid or tripod above the
fire. You don't want it to
get too hot underneath,
which can burn the fruit.**

**Because it has a lid, a Dutch oven is perfect for making
this comforting campfire dessert. You can place some of
the hot embers from the fire on top, so you end up with an
appetisingly golden brown, crunchy cobbler. If you don't
have a Dutch oven, use a cast-iron pan and cover with a lid.**

1. If you're cooking this over a campfire, let it burn down to
   the embers and place a grill grate over them.
2. Make the cobbler topping: mix the flour, baking powder,
   sugar and salt together in a bowl. Rub in the softened
   butter with your fingertips and then stir in the milk until you
   have a soft dough. If it's too crumbly, add a little more milk.
3. Put the fruit, sugar, cinnamon and cornflour in a ziplock
   plastic bag and shake well until the fruit is lightly coated.
4. Line a Dutch oven with parchment paper or a paper liner
   and smear with butter. Add the fruit mixture and then drop
   spoonfuls of the cobbler mixture on top, leaving spaces in
   between. Sprinkle lightly with sugar and cover with the lid.
5. Place over the fire and put some glowing hot coals on the
   lid. Cook for 35–45 minutes or until the fruit is bubbling and
   the topping is cooked through and golden brown. Cool a
   little before serving.

Variations
• Use drained tinned peaches and apricots, or cut up some
  windfall apples, plums or pears.
• Instead of using butter and milk in the cobbler, stir 150ml
  (¼ pint/generous ½ cup) double (heavy) cream into the dry
  flour mixture.
• Serve with cream or ready-made custard.

ALL FIRED UP

BBQ & FIRE PIT FOOD

STICKY-GLAZED BBQ RIBS

SERVES 4–6 | PREP 20 MINUTES | CHILL 1 HOUR | COOK 1½ – 2 HOURS

2 x 1.5kg (3lb 5oz) racks of
   pork ribs, trimmed of
   excess fat
4 tbsp paprika
2 tsp dried thyme or oregano
2 tsp sea salt
freshly ground black pepper

BBQ glaze
240ml (8fl oz/1 cup) tomato
   ketchup
120ml (4fl oz/½ cup) hoisin
   sauce
50g dark soft brown sugar
3 tbsp soy sauce
1 tbsp cider vinegar

Tip:
**These ribs cook well and
have a wonderful smoky
flavour if you have a kettle
barbecue or one with a lid.**

**Tender and juicy on the inside and sticky and aromatic on
the outside, smoky BBQ ribs are sure to please everyone.
If you're off-grid out in the wilds and don't have a
barbecue, you can cook them on a grill laid over the
glowing hot coals and embers of a campfire.**

1. If you're cooking this over a campfire, let it burn down to
   the embers and place a grill grate over them. If you're using
   a barbecue, heat it to medium.
2. Sprinkle the ribs with the paprika, dried herbs and salt.
   Grind over some black pepper. Place on a foil-lined baking
   sheet, cover and leave in a fridge, cooler or a cool place for
   at least 1 hour, preferably 4 hours.
3. Mix together all the ingredients for the BBQ glaze in a bowl.
4. Once the flames have died down and the barbecue or fire is
   hot, push the hot coals towards the sides so they won't be
   directly under the ribs while they are cooking.
5. Brush some of the glaze over a large sheet of foil and place
   the ribs on top. Brush more glaze over the ribs and then pull
   up the foil and seal the edges to make a loose parcel. Place
   on the grill and cook for 1½–2 hours, rotating them and
   brushing with glaze every 30 minutes, until they are cooked
   right through and tender. Uncover them at the end so they
   are nicely browned.
6. Separate the ribs and serve immediately with baked
   potatoes and salad.

Variations
• Add some Chinese five-spice powder, grated fresh ginger or
  garlic to the glaze.
• You can use honey or maple syrup instead of sugar.

BBQ QUARTER POUNDERS

SERVES 4 | PREP 10 MINUTES | COOK 6–12 MINUTES

500g (1lb 2oz/2¼ cups)
   minced (ground) lean beef
   (10% fat)
½ red onion, grated
a few drops of Worcestershire
   sauce
4 burger buns
a handful of crisp Cos
   (Romaine) lettuce, torn
   into pieces
2 ripe tomatoes, sliced
sea salt and freshly ground
   black pepper
Quick & Easy BBQ Sauce (see
   page 28), tomato ketchup or
   mustard, to serve

Tip:
For cheeseburgers, place a
slice of cheese on top of the
burger as soon as you turn
it over on the grill and cook
the other side (as per step
4 above).

Juicy beef burgers taste best when cooked over a campfire
or on a charcoal BBQ. This gives them a delicious charred
and smoky flavour. When you're camping, it's important to
keep fresh meat as cold as possible, so if you don't have a
portable fridge use a cooler.

1. If you're cooking this over a campfire, let it burn down to
   the embers and place a grill grate over them. Heat the
   barbecue to medium until the flames die down and it's hot.
2. Meanwhile, mix the minced beef and grated onion in a bowl.
   Add the Worcestershire sauce and a little salt and pepper.
3. Divide the mixture into four equal-sized portions and,
   mould each one into a burger, flattening them slightly.
4. Place the burgers on the grill above the hot coals and cook
   for 3–4 minutes. Turn them over carefully and cook for
   3–4 minutes (rare); 5–6 minutes (medium); or 7 minutes
   (well done). Remove and set aside to rest for 2–3 minutes.
5. Meanwhile, split the burger buns and place them, cut-side
   down, on the barbecue grill. Toast for 2–3 minutes.
6. Remove and place the lettuce and tomatoes on the base of
   each bun. Add the burgers and drizzle with the BBQ Sauce,
   tomato ketchup or mustard. Cover with the lids and serve
   immediately.

Variations
• Add some celery salt, garlic powder, dried herbs, crushed
  dried chilli flakes or some chopped fresh parsley or thyme
  to the burger mix.
• Instead of buns, use wholemeal or granary rolls, warmed
  split muffins or pitta breads, or even wraps.

 **ALL FIRED UP**

GRILLED HALLOUMI BURGERS

SERVES 4 | PREP 15 MINUTES | COOK 8–10 MINUTES

4 large field or portobello
    mushrooms
olive oil, for brushing
400g (14oz) halloumi, cut into
    thick slices
4 seeded burger buns
a handful of rocket (arugula),
    baby spinach or crisp
    lettuce
1 large beefsteak tomato, cut
    into 4 slices
½ red onion, thinly sliced
sea salt and freshly ground
    black pepper
tomato ketchup, mayonnaise
    or fruity chutney, to serve

Tip:
**Halloumi is great for
camping because it keeps
well for weeks (or even
months) in a cool place if
it's left sealed in brine in its
original packaging.**

Halloumi tastes especially good and acquires a lovely smoky flavour when it's cooked over hot coals or wood on a barbecue or fire pit. It's not called the 'grilling cheese' for nothing. Unlike most other cheeses, it has a very high melting point and you can griddle, grill, fry or barbecue it without it melting or losing its shape.

1. If you're cooking this over a campfire, let it burn down to the embers and place a grill grate over them. If you're using a barbecue, heat it to medium.
2. Brush the mushrooms with oil, season with salt and pepper, and place them on the barbecue grill or a grate set over the fire. Cook for 6–8 minutes, turning them halfway through, until tender and golden brown.
3. Meanwhile, brush the halloumi lightly with oil. Place on the hot grill and cook for 2–3 minutes each side until it's appetisingly golden brown and slightly crisp and charred.
4. Brush the cut sides of the burgers buns and grill for about 2–3 minutes.
5. Place a mushroom on the base of each bun and fill with the salad leaves. Layer the sliced tomato and halloumi on top, finishing with the red onion and the sauce of your choice, e.g. ketchup, mayo or chutney. Cover with the top half of the bun and eat immediately while the halloumi is still hot.

Variations
• Marinate the halloumi before grilling (see page 44).
• For a spicy take on this, sprinkle the halloumi with jerk seasoning before grilling.
• Add some sliced avocado or grilled aubergine (eggplant).

ALL FIRED UP 101

EMBER-COOKED 'DIRTY' STEAKS

SERVES 4 | PREP 10 MINUTES | COOK 40–50 MINUTES

4 large red onions, skins on

4 uncooked beetroot (beets), unpeeled

4 thick-cut rump or sirloin steaks, at least 2.5cm (1in) thick

olive oil, for brushing and drizzling

balsamic vinegar, for drizzling

seasoning or rub of your choice (see pages 29–31) (optional)

2 large handfuls of rocket (arugula) or watercress

2–3 tbsp salad dressing of your choice (see pages 35–6)

sea salt and freshly ground black pepper

Dijon mustard, to serve

Tip:
You can also cook this on a grill grate placed just above the embers of the fire.

Cooking food in the glowing embers of the fire goes back to prehistoric times. It's as close to nature as it gets and is known as 'dirty cooking'. You will need lots of hot charcoal to generate sufficient intense heat but it's worth it to enjoy a really smoky and juicy 'dirty' steak. When handling the food on the fire, wear heatproof gloves and use long-handled tongs.

1. Light your fire or barbecue in advance and wait for the early flames to die down and for it to get hot with really glowing coals and embers. Flatten out the coals so the meat has maximum contact with them.

2. Place the unpeeled onions and beetroot among the hot coals and cook in their skins for about 40 minutes, turning them occasionally, until they are cooked and tender inside and blackened on the outside.

3. Using tongs, remove the red onions and beetroot and place on a wooden board. Brush off any ash and set aside to cool for at least 5 minutes before peeling off the blackened skins. Cut into quarters or wedges and drizzle with olive oil and balsamic vinegar. Season with salt and pepper and set aside while you cook the steaks.

4. Season the steaks with a seasoning or rub, or just salt and pepper, and place them directly on the hot coals – choose somewhere with the least ash. Cook for 2 minutes each side for rare to medium rare; 4 minutes for medium to well done.

5. Remove the steaks and rest for at least 2 minutes before cutting into slices. Serve with the red onions, beetroot and rocket or watercress tossed in the dressing, with some mustard on the side.

STICKY SAUSAGE HOT DOGS

SERVES 4 | PREP 10 MINUTES | COOK 15–20 MINUTES

4 good-quality large pork
   sausages
1 tbsp Dijon mustard, plus
   extra to serve
2 tbsp runny honey
1 tbsp soy sauce
4 hot dog rolls (buns)
tomato ketchup, to serve

Tips:
**You can lightly grill
the rolls (buns) to
warm them through,
if wished.**

**You can also set up
a rack or grill grate
resting on some bricks
over a campfire and
grill the skewered hot
dogs over the glowing
coals, turning them
occasionally.**

**Nothing beats sweet, smoky and sticky charred sausages
cooked on the barbecue or a bonfire. They are so easy to
prepare and cook, and the ultimate finger food. Enjoy with
salad and a cold beer on a warm evening, or with mulled
wine or cider on a cold night.**

1. Heat the barbecue to medium until the flames die down
   and it's hot (or see tip if you are cooking on a campfire).
2. Take two long wooden skewers that have been soaked
   in cold water to prevent them burning. Thread all the
   sausages on to one of the skewers, pushing it through
   them on their right sides. Then push the other skewers
   through them on their left sides, so you end up with them
   threaded on two parallel skewers. This will make it easier to
   baste and turn them while they are cooking.
3. Mix together the mustard, honey and soy sauce.
4. Place the sausages on the hot barbecue grill and brush with
   the honey mustard glaze. Cook, turning them occasionally
   and brushing them frequently with the glaze, for 15–20
   minutes, or until cooked through, sticky and starting to char.
5. Split the bread rolls and place a sausage in each one. Drizzle
   with tomato ketchup and mustard and serve immediately.

Variations
- Serve with fruity chutney, relish or apple sauce.
- Substitute hot sauce or sweet chilli sauce for the ketchup.
- Top the sausages with some grilled sliced red onions or
  charred grilled red (bell) peppers.
- Add a dash of Worcestershire sauce, harissa or garlic paste
  to the glaze.

STICKY BBQ CHICKEN & PINEAPPLE KEBABS

SERVES 4 | PREP 15 MINUTES | MARINATE 30 MINUTES | COOK 15 MINUTES

4 chicken breasts, cut into
chunks

2 red, green or yellow (bell)
peppers, deseeded and cut
into chunks

2 small red onions, cut into
wedges

1 ripe small pineapple,
peeled, cored and cut into
chunks

baked potatoes, warm
flatbreads or couscous,
to serve

Sticky glaze

4 tbsp olive oil

3 tbsp runny honey

3 tbsp soy sauce

juice of 1 lime

3 garlic cloves, crushed

What's not to like about these sticky chicken kebabs? You can prepare them in advance and leave them to marinate while you sit by the warming fire or grill and enjoy a pre-supper drink. If you don't have a barbecue, cook them on a rack or grill grate over the fire, or even in a griddle pan on the camping stove.

1. Heat the barbecue on the medium setting until the flames die down and it's hot.
2. Make the sticky glaze: stir all the ingredients together in a bowl until well blended. Add the chicken and stir until coated all over. Cover and leave to marinate in a cool place for at least 30 minutes.
3. Thread the marinated chicken, peppers, red onion and pineapple onto four long or eight short wooden (soaked in water first) or metal skewers. Lightly brush the vegetables and pineapple with any leftover glaze.
4. Place on the hot barbecue grill and cook, turning them occasionally and brushing them frequently with the glaze, for about 15 minutes, or until the chicken is cooked through and starting to char.
5. Serve immediately with some baked potatoes, flatbreads or couscous.

Variations

• This also works well with pork fillet or large prawns (jumbo shrimp).
• Vary the vegetables: try courgettes (zucchini), cherry tomatoes, baby corn, aubergine (eggplant) and mushrooms.
• Serve with a crisp green salad or some guacamole.

 **108** ALL FIRED UP

SOUVLAKIA

SERVES 4–6 | PREP 10 MINUTES | MARINATE 30 MINUTES | COOK 12–15 MINUTES

12 boneless chicken thighs,
    skinned, cut into large
    chunks
4 flatbreads
sea salt and freshly ground
    black pepper
Greek yoghurt or tahini
    and Dukkah (see page 32),
    to serve

Marinade

5 tbsp olive oil
juice of ½ lemon
4 garlic cloves, crushed
2 tsp dried oregano
1 tsp dried mint
a few crushed dried chilli
    flakes or a pinch of
    cayenne pepper

Tip:
If using wooden skewers,
soak them in cold water
first to prevent them
burning.

We have used chicken in this recipe but you can substitute lean steak, lamb or pork fillet (tenderloin) or large prawns (jumbo shrimp). Alternatively, you can make a vegetarian version with skewered wedges of aubergine (eggplant), pumpkin, squash or even tofu or halloumi.

1. Heat the barbecue on the medium setting until the flames die down and it's hot.
2. Make the marinade: mix together all the ingredients in a bowl with some salt and pepper. Add the chicken thighs and turn them in the marinade. Cover and leave in a cool place for at least 30 minutes.
3. Thread the chicken onto four long or eight short wooden or metal skewers. Press the pieces of chicken tightly together with no gaps in between.
4. When the barbecue is really hot and the coals turn ashen, lay the kebabs on the grill and cook, turning occasionally and brushing with leftover marinade, for 12–15 minutes or until the chicken is cooked right through and golden brown.
5. Towards the end, place the flatbreads on the grill and toast for about 2 minutes each side to warm them through.
6. Serve the kebabs with the yoghurt or tahini sprinkled with dukkah (if using), and the warm flatbreads.

Variations

• Remove the grilled chicken and vegetables from the skewers and place on wraps smeared with yoghurt, tahini or tzatziki. Add some salad and roll up.
• Alternatively, stuff them into some split warmed pitta.

ALL FIRED UP **109**

BBQ BAKED FISH PARCELS

SERVES 4 | PREP 15 MINUTES | COOK 20–30 MINUTES

4 x 250g (9oz) small whole
   fish, e.g. red or grey mullet,
   mackerel, sea bass or trout,
   scaled, gutted and cleaned
a bunch of parsley
fine sea salt and freshly
   ground black pepper
lemon juice and fruity green
   olive oil, to serve

Tip:
Don't worry if the
newspaper gets very black
and charred. You can damp
it down with more water.
When it starts to burn,
it's time to turn it over or
remove it.

This is a great way of cooking fish on a barbecue or on a
grid laid over the glowing hot embers of an open fire. The
beauty of this simple method is that the fish steams inside
the paper parcel in its own juices. You will need plenty of
newspaper to make this delicious dish.

1. If you're cooking this over a campfire, let it burn down to
   the embers and place a grill grate over them. If you're using
   a barbecue, heat it on the medium setting until the flames
   die down and it's hot.
2. Sprinkle some sea salt all over each fish and inside the
   cavity. Add a grinding of black pepper and stuff each one
   with parsley.
3. Dampen some sheets of newspaper with water. Wrap each
   fish in five sheets to enclose it securely and make a parcel.
4. Place the paper-wrapped fish on the barbecue or on a grill
   above the hot coals. Cook for 10 minutes, then carefully
   turn them over and cook for 10 minutes on the other side.
   If you are using larger fish – say, 2 x 500g (1lb 2oz) – cook for
   about 15 minutes each side.
5. Gently remove the cooked fish from the paper – most
   of the skin will stick to it and peel away neatly, leaving a
   perfectly cooked fish.
6. Drizzle some lemon juice and olive oil over the succulent
   flesh and remove the bones as you eat.

Variations
• Put a slice of lemon inside each fish before wrapping and
  cooking it.
• Serve with a salad or some boiled or stir-fried greens.

ALL FIRED UP

GREEK-STYLE CHARCOAL-GRILLED LAMB

SERVES 4 | PREP 10 MINUTES | MARINATE 1 HOUR | COOK 4–8 MINUTES

5 tbsp olive oil

juice of 1 lemon

3 garlic cloves, crushed

2 tsp dried oregano

8 lamb chops or cutlets

sea salt and freshly ground
    black pepper

lemon wedges, to serve

Quick tzatziki

200g (7oz/scant 1 cup) Greek
    yoghurt

½ cucumber, diced

1 garlic clove, crushed

a handful of mint, chopped

Tip:
You can marinate and grill
lamb steaks in the same way.

There's no better way to eat lamb than this – cooked on the barbecue (or on a grill grate set over an open fire) and infused with the smoky aroma of charcoal or wood.

1. If you're cooking this over a campfire, let it burn down to the embers and place a grill grate over them. If you're using a barbecue, heat it on the high setting until the flames die down and it's hot.
2. Mix together the olive oil, lemon juice, garlic and dried oregano in a bowl with some salt and pepper. Add the lamb chops and turn them in the marinade. Cover and leave in a cool place for at least 1 hour.
3. Meanwhile, make the tzatziki: mix everything together in a bowl. Season to taste with salt and pepper, then cover and set aside for the flavours to infuse.
4. When the barbecue is really hot and the coals turn ashen, cook the lamb on the grill for 2–4 minutes each side, brushing with any leftover marinade. If you like your lamb really pink and rare, 2 minutes per side will be enough – cook longer for medium or well done.
5. Serve immediately with lemon wedges for squeezing and tzatziki on the side.

Variations
• Use dried mint in the tzatziki if you don't have any fresh.
• Add some fennel seeds and finely diced fennel bulb to the tzatziki.
• Serve with tinned white beans, onion and tomatoes in a lemony vinaigrette.
• Serve with warmed pittas or flatbreads.

ALL-IN-ONE BBQ FAJITAS

SERVES 4 | PREP 15 MINUTES | COOK 10–15 MINUTES

olive oil, for brushing and
  drizzling
4 chicken breasts, skinless,
  cut into strips
1 red (bell) pepper, deseeded
  and cut into strips
1 green (bell) pepper, deseeded
  and cut into strips
1 yellow (bell) pepper,
  deseeded and cut into strips
2 onions (white or red), thinly
  sliced
1–2 chillies, diced
8 large corn or flour tortillas
a handful of coriander
  (cilantro), chopped
sea salt and freshly ground
  black pepper
salsa, Pico de Gallo (see page
  46), Guacamole (see page 40),
  soured cream, hot sauce and
  lime wedges, to serve

Tip:
These parcels can also be
cooked in the glowing hot
coals of a campfire. They
will take 15–20 minutes.

This is an easy way to cook fajitas on the barbeuce –
there's less mess and nothing falls through the bars. It's
a very versatile dish and you can add almost anything
you like to the packets. For a really authentic Mexican
flavour, dust the chicken and vegetables with some fajita
seasoning (available from most supermarkets and delis).

1. Heat the barbecue on the medium to medium-high setting
   until the flames die down and it's hot.
2. Meanwhile, take four 30 x 30cm (12 x 12in) squares of
   kitchen foil and brush lightly with oil. Divide the chicken,
   peppers, onion and chilli between them. Season with salt
   and pepper and drizzle with olive oil.
3. Bring the sides of each square of foil up into the centre and
   twist them together to make a sealed parcel.
4. When the barbecue is hot, place the parcels on the grill and,
   if you have one, cover with the lid. Don't worry if you don't
   – it might just take a little longer to cook. Cook for about
   10–15 minutes, until the chicken is cooked right through
   and the vegetables are tender.
5. Warm the tortillas on the barbecue for 1–2 minutes each
   side. Open the foil packets and sprinkle with coriander.
   Give everyone their own packet and tortillas so they can
   assemble the fajitas.
6. Divide the chicken and vegetables among the tortillas
   and top with Pico de Gallo, Guacamole or soured cream, a
   drizzle of hot sauce and a squeeze of lime. Roll up or fold
   them over and eat in your hands.

CAMPFIRE GRILLED CHICKEN 3 WAYS

SERVES 4 | PREP 5–10 MINUTES | COOK 16–20 MINUTES

4 chicken breasts or 8 legs, on the bone with skin
olive oil, for brushing
sea salt and freshly ground black pepper

Wholegrain mustard glaze

2 tbsp wholegrain mustard

Sticky honey glaze

2 tbsp runny honey
2 tbsp light soy sauce
1 garlic clove, crushed

Teriyaki glaze

60ml (2fl oz/¼ cup) teriyaki sauce
juice of 1 lemon
2 garlic cloves, crushed
2 tsp sesame or light olive oil

Tip:
The flavour of the teriyaki chicken will be more intense if you marinate it in the glaze for 30 minutes before grilling.

As good as it gets … chicken simply cooked out of doors over the glowing embers of a campfire or the hot coals of a barbecue. This is the oldest cooking method of all and probably the best. Eat it plain with a little herb butter or try one of the following suggestions. They are all quick, easy and delicious.

1. Light the fire and wait for the embers to glow grey and ashy, or heat the barbecue on the high setting until the flames die down and it's hot. If cooking over the open fire, place the chicken on a grill grate above the glowing embers and cook as above.
2. If cooking the chicken plain, just brush with olive oil and season with salt and pepper.
3. Or brush with oil and then the mustard.
4. Or mix together the honey, soy sauce and garlic and brush over the chicken.
5. Or mix together the ingredients for the teriyaki glaze and brush over the chicken.
6. When the barbecue is really hot and the coals turn ashen, lightly oil the barbecue grill or grate and place the chicken on top. Cook for 8–10 minutes on each side until the chicken is cooked right through and the juices run clear when you pierce it with a skewer or fork.
7. Remove the chicken and eat immediately with a baked potato and some salad or grilled vegetables.

FIRE-BAKED POTATOES

SERVES 4 | PREP 5 MINUTES | COOK 30–45 MINUTES

4 medium baking potatoes, washed
4 tbsp softened butter, plus extra to serve
sea salt crystals or flakes and freshly ground black pepper

Tip:
You can cook the foil-wrapped potatoes on the barbecue or grill. Instead of puncturing the potatoes before wrapping them, pierce with a skewer right through the foil several times. Cook on a hot grill, turning occasionally, for 1 hour or until soft.

The easiest supper of all when you're on a camping trip and craving fuss-free delicious food. Nearly everyone loves baked potatoes and you can cook them to perfection in the glowing embers of the fire pit or campfire. You can cook sweet potatoes in exactly the same way.

1. If you're cooking this over a campfire, let it burn down until you have really glowing coals and embers.
2. Pierce each potato two or three times on each side with a fork. Smear with butter and place on a large square of kitchen foil. Sprinkle with sea salt and wrap securely in the foil before wrapping in a second piece of foil.
3. Put the potatoes in among the hot coals and ashes, and cook for 30–45 minutes until soft and cooked right through. They may need longer, depending on the heat of the fire.
4. Remove with hot tongs and be careful when opening the foil packets and splitting the potatoes – they will be very hot and steamy! Serve with plenty of butter and salt and pepper or one of the toppings below.

Toppings
• Sprinkle with grated cheese and crispy bacon.
• Add a dollop of yoghurt or soured cream and some chopped chives or parsley.
• Top with baked beans or some chilli (minced beef or vegetarian).
• Add a spoonful of coleslaw and some grated Cheddar.
• Top with hummus or Baba Ghanoush (see page 118).
• Add some tuna mayo and chopped spring onions (scallions).

7

SPEEDY SIDES & SALADS

BABA GHANOUSH

SERVES 4 | PREP 5 MINUTES | COOK 30 MINUTES

2 large aubergines (eggplants)
2 garlic cloves, crushed
juice of 1 lemon
2 tbsp olive oil, plus extra
　for drizzling
a few sprigs of flat-leaf
　parsley or mint, chopped
pomegranate seeds or toasted
　pine nuts, for sprinkling
sea salt and freshly ground
　black pepper
grilled flatbreads, pitta or
　toast, to serve

This smoky aubergine (eggplant) purée is so versatile and is a great accompaniment for grilled meat, sausages, chicken, fish and vegetables. You can also eat it as a dip or a spread.

1. If you're cooking this over a campfire, let it burn down to the embers and place a grill grate over them. If you're using a barbecue, heat it to medium.
2. Prick the aubergines all over with the point of a knife (this will stop them bursting open). Cook over hot coals on the barbecue or on a grate set over the fire, turning them occasionally, for about 30 minutes, or until they are really charred all over and so soft that they lose their shape and start to collapse. Set aside to cool.
3. Skin the aubergines or cut them in half and scoop out the soft flesh. Chop it roughly or mash with a fork. Mix in a bowl with the garlic, lemon juice, olive oil and herbs. Season with salt and pepper.
4. Serve, drizzled with olive oil and sprinkled with pomegranate seeds or pine nuts, with warm flatbreads, pitta or toast.

Variations
- Add 1–2 tablespoons tahini.
- Spice it up with ground cumin, chilli powder or cayenne.
- Dust lightly with smoked or sweet paprika.
- Stir in some diced grilled (bell) peppers or tomatoes.

FOIL-ROASTED FENNEL, TOMATOES & GREENS

SERVES 4 | PREP 15 MINUTES | COOK 30 MINUTES

1 large fennel bulb, trimmed
and sliced
2 red onions, cut into wedges
500g (1lb 2oz) cherry tomatoes
on the vine
500g (1lb 2oz) spinach or
kale, washed, trimmed and
coarsely chopped
fruity green olive oil, for
drizzling
crushed dried chilli flakes,
for sprinkling
sea salt and freshly ground
black pepper

Campfire cooking doesn't get simpler than this. Just put all the ingredients in a foil tray or container and cook over the campfire or a barbecue until deliciously charred and tender. You can cook almost any vegetables in this way.

1. If you're cooking this over a campfire, let it burn down to the embers and place a grill grate over them. If you're using a barbecue, heat it to medium.
2. Spread out the fennel, onion wedges, tomatoes and greens on one large or two medium foil trays or containers. Drizzle with plenty of olive oil – don't be coy – and sprinkle with 1 or 2 pinches of chilli flakes and some salt and pepper. Cover loosely with some kitchen foil.
3. Place over the hot coals on the barbecue grill or on a grate or tripod over the glowing embers of the campfire and cook for about 20 minutes. Uncover and turn the vegetables over in the oil. Cook for another 10 minutes or so, until they are tender, smoky and slightly charred.
4. Serve hot with grilled fish or chicken, or tofu or halloumi.

Variations
• Drizzle with syrupy balsamic vinegar or some lemon juice.
• Serve with creamy goat's cheese or some sliced feta.
• Sprinkle with toasted pine nuts or sesame seeds.

BBQ SWEET POTATO & FETA SALAD

SERVES 4 | PREP 15 MINUTES | COOK 15 MINUTES

2 large sweet potatoes,
  scrubbed and thickly sliced
2–3 tbsp fruity green olive
  oil, plus extra for brushing
1 small red onion, finely
  chopped
300g (10oz) baby plum or
  cherry tomatoes, chopped
1 bag ready-washed baby leaf
  spinach or rocket (arugula)
juice of ½ lemon
150g (5oz) feta cheese,
  crumbled or diced
balsamic vinegar or
  pomegranate molasses,
  for drizzling
sea salt and freshly ground
  black pepper

Tip:
**You can wrap the whole
sweet potatoes in kitchen
foil and cook them in the
glowing embers of the
barbecue or a campfire and
then scoop out the flesh
and mix with the other
salad ingredients.**

**Most vegetables can be grilled on the barbecue and then
tossed in a dressing with other salad ingredients. To make
this into a more substantial meal, stir everything into
some cooked brown rice, couscous, quinoa or other grains.**

1. If you're cooking this over a campfire, let it burn down to
   the embers and place a grill grate over them. If you're using
   a barbecue, heat it to medium.
2. Brush the sweet potato slices on both sides with some
   olive oil and place on the barbecue grill above the hot coals
   or on a grill grate over the glowing embers of the fire. Cook
   for about 8 minutes each side, or until they are slightly
   charred and tender but keep their shape.
3. Mix together the onion, tomatoes and spinach or rocket in
   a bowl. Add the sweet potatoes and season with salt and
   pepper.
4. Stir the olive oil and lemon juice together or shake in a
   screwtop jar until blended. Pour over the salad and toss
   together gently.
5. Sprinkle the feta over the top, then drizzle with balsamic
   vinegar or pomegranate molasses and serve while the
   sweet potato is still warm.

Variations
• Add some diced chilli, sesame seeds or chopped herbs.
• Instead of feta, serve with torn mozzarella or grilled halloumi.
• Toss in one of the dressings on pages 35–6.
• Add some grilled red or yellow (bell) peppers or aubergines
  (eggplants).

MEXICAN-STYLE GRILLED SWEETCORN

SERVES 4 | PREP 10 MINUTES | COOK 10–15 MINUTES

4 large cobs (ears) sweetcorn,
  husks removed
oil, for brushing
sea salt and freshly ground
  black pepper

Chilli lime butter

50g (2oz/¼ cup) butter,
  softened
1 garlic clove, crushed
grated zest and juice of 1 lime
a handful of coriander
  (cilantro), finely chopped
1 hot red chilli, deseeded
  and diced

Variations

- Use 1 teaspoon chilli powder
  or ground chipotle pepper
  instead of fresh chilli.
- Or use crushed dried chilli
  or red pepper flakes.
- If you don't have chilli, use
  some sriracha or sweet
  chilli sauce.
- Alternatively, instead of
  using butter, mix the garlic,
  lime, herbs and chilli with
  some mayo and use as a dip.

In Mexico, corn-on-the-cobs are often cooked in this way and served slathered with chilli butter and sprinkled with crumbled Cotija cheese. If you want to try eating it this way, feta makes a good substitute.

1. Preheat the barbecue on medium-high heat.
2. Make the chilli lime butter: mix all the ingredients together in a bowl.
3. Lightly oil the grate of the hot barbecue and place the corn cobs on top. Cook, turning frequently, for 10–15 minutes, until the cobs are tender, starting to char and golden brown all over.
4. Serve the hot corn immediately topped with the chilli lime butter.

Note:
Corn also cooks to smoky perfection over the hot embers of a campfire. Don't remove the husks – they make a good natural covering, protecting the juicy, succulent corn inside while it cooks. Soak them in cold water for 30 minutes before cooking to soften the husks. Remove, pat dry and peel back the husks, leaving them attached to the base of the corn, and remove the silky threads inside. Pull up the husks to cover the corn and then cook on a grate over the embers. Alternatively, wrap some husked corn cobs in foil and place on the grate.

GARLICKY CAMPFIRE POTATOES

SERVES 4 | PREP 10 MINUTES | COOK 30–40 MINUTES

900g (2lb) small new potatoes
4 tbsp olive oil
4–6 garlic cloves, crushed
a good pinch of crushed dried
   chilli or red pepper flakes
1 tsp chopped rosemary,
   thyme or oregano
sea salt and freshly ground
   black pepper

Caution!
Be careful when opening
the hot foil parcels. They
will be full of hot steam.
It's a good idea to pierce
the foil before opening to
release the steam.

Who doesn't like potatoes, and the good news is that they are so easy to cook on a fire or a barbecue. Just wrap them in foil and forget about them for half an hour. They taste great with grilled steaks, chicken, chops and fish.

1. If you're cooking this over a campfire, let it burn down to the embers and place a grill grate over them. If you're using a barbecue, heat it to medium.
2. Take four large squares of kitchen foil and divide the potatoes among them. Lift the edges of the foil up around the potatoes towards the centre and then drizzle the oil over them. Add the garlic, chilli flakes, herbs and a good grinding of sea salt and black pepper.
3. Seal the foil parcels to enclose the potatoes securely but loosely, twisting the edges of the foil together and crimping them between your fingers.
4. Place the packages on the barbecue grill or a grate set just above the hot coals and cook for 30–40 minutes, moving them occasionally, until the potatoes are tender.

Variations
- Add some grated lemon zest and a squeeze of juice.
- If you don't have fresh herbs, sprinkle the potatoes with dried ones.
- If you don't have fresh garlic, use garlic salt.
- Add some grated Parmesan cheese.
- You could even add some capers, anchovy fillets or chopped spring onions (scallions).

GRILLED MUSHROOMS WITH GARLIC & HERBS

SERVES 4 | PREP 15 MINUTES | COOK 15 MINUTES

8 large field or portobello
   mushrooms, thickly sliced
3–4 tbsp olive oil
4 garlic cloves, crushed
½ tsp dried oregano or
   marjoram
a handful of parsley or chives,
   chopped
sea salt and freshly ground
   black pepper

Tip:
**Instead of wrapping the
mushrooms in a foil parcel,
leave them whole and fill
with the garlic, herbs and
oil. Brush the outer edges
with oil and cook on the
grill until tender.**

Variations
• Use smaller chestnut or
  button mushrooms, or
  foraged mushrooms. Leave
  whole or cut in half or into
  quarters.
• Drizzle a little soy sauce or
  balsamic vinegar over the
  cooked mushrooms.

**These garlicky mushrooms are surprisingly filling and are
delicious with grilled chicken, sausages and steaks. Vegans
can enjoy them with chargrilled sliced tofu, vegeburgers or
Sloppy Joes (see page 87). These also cook well wrapped in
foil in the ashy embers of a fire.**

1. If you're cooking this over a campfire, let it burn down to
   the embers and place a grill grate over them. If you're using
   a barbecue, heat until it's really hot.
2. Place the mushrooms in the centre of a large rectangular
   sheet of kitchen foil, leaving at least 2.5cm (1in) around the
   edge. Sprinkle with olive oil, the crushed garlic and dried
   herbs. Season with salt and pepper.
3. Place another sheet of foil over the top and twist the edges
   securely together to seal the package. Pierce the top a few
   times with a skewer and place on the barbecue above the
   hot coals or in the ashy embers of the fire.
4. Cover the barbecue with the lid if it has one and cook
   for 10 minutes, then turn the package over and cook for
   5 minutes, or until the mushrooms are tender.
5. Remove from the heat and carefully open the foil parcel.
   Sprinkle with chopped parsley or chives and serve
   immediately.

DRINK UP

COCKTAILS, MOCKTAILS, COOLERS & WARMERS

SANGRIA

MAKES 1.3 LITRES (2¼ PINTS/SCANT 6 CUPS) | PREP 10 MINUTES

750ml (1¼ pints/generous
   3 cups) red wine (1 bottle)
60ml (2fl oz/¼ cup) brandy
2–3 tbsp caster (superfine)
   sugar
2 juicy oranges, sliced or cut
   into pieces
500ml (17fl oz/generous
   2 cups) soda water or
   sparkling water
ice cubes, to serve.

This Spanish fruit punch is a refreshing drink for warm summer days. It's easy to make and you can use any dry or medium red wine. Serve it with a dip, a bowl of potato or tortilla chips or nibbles, or even some tapas, e.g. diced chorizo and olives.

1. Pour the wine and brandy into a large jug (pitcher). Stir in the sugar to dissolve it and then add the oranges.
2. Top up with the soda water or sparkling water. Give it a good stir and serve in tall glasses with ice.

Variations
- If you don't have red wine, use rosé.
- Vary the spirits: try rum, Cointreau or Grand Marnier.
- For a less sweet version, omit the sugar, and use 1 lemon and 1 orange.
- For a really sweet version, top up with lemonade, not water.
- To make it more colourful, add sliced peaches or apples, strawberries, raspberries or diced melon.

CAMPING TINTO DE VERANO

MAKES 1.5 LITRES (3½ PINTS/6 CUPS) | PREP 5 MINUTES

750ml (1¼ pints/generous
    3 cups) red wine (1 bottle)
750ml (1¼ pints/generous
    3 cups) lemonade
1 lemon, thinly sliced
ice cubes, to serve

Note:
For a lighter version, use
1 part red wine to 2 parts
lemonade. Don't use a fine
wine for this – a simple
table wine will suffice.

This simpler take on sangria is the beloved summer drink
of most Spaniards. It's so quick and easy to make – just red
wine and lemonade. Depending on where you fall on the
sweetness spectrum, you can choose from pink lemonade,
Sprite, lemon Fanta and 7-Up to bitter lemon. And if you
don't like it sweet, use soda water instead.

1. Pour the wine into a large jug (pitcher). Add the lemonade
   and sliced lemon and stir well.
2. Pour into tall glasses and serve with ice.

Variations
• Add a splash of red vermouth.
• Use a mixture of lemonade and soda water or a lemon-
   flavoured sparkling water.
• Add sliced orange as well as lemon.

STRAWBERRY LEMONADE COOLER

SERVES 1 | PREP 5 MINUTES

6 ripe strawberries, hulled
   and chopped
150ml (¼ pint/generous
   ½ cup) lemonade
150ml (¼ pint/generous
   ½ cup) soda water
ice cubes and fresh mint,
   to serve

This is a simple basic camping version of a classic mocktail. Usually the strawberries are puréed by blitzing them in a blender, but when you're in the great outdoors or off-grid, mashing them with a fork will suffice. This is a great way of using up really ripe strawberries! The quantities below are for one serving – just double or quadruple, as required.

1. Mash the strawberries in a tall glass with a fork or wooden spoon.
2. Pour in the lemonade and soda water and mix well. Add some ice and sprigs of mint, and enjoy.

Variations
- Use limeade instead of lemonade.
- If you don't have soda water, use sparkling water or tonic water.
- Vary the berries: try raspberries or blueberries.
- You could even add some ginger beer.
- Top with some sliced strawberries.

SMOKY CAMPFIRE MARGARITAS

SERVES 1 | PREP 10 MINUTES

fine sea salt, for the glass

2 tbsp fresh lime juice, plus
   extra for the glass

45ml (1½fl oz/3 tbsp) tequila

15ml (½oz/1 tbsp) mezcal

15ml (½oz/1 tbsp) maple
   syrup

a dash of orange bitters
   (optional)

1 drop of liquid smoke
   (optional)

ice cubes, to serve

This is the perfect summer's evening cocktail by the grill or the fire. Using smoked salt or liquid smoke, if you have it, will transform a classic margarita into a campfire special.

1. Spread a little sea salt out on a saucer. Dampen the rim of a glass with lime juice and dip it lightly into the salt so it sticks and forms a salty edge.
2. Mix the lime juice, tequila, mezcal and maple syrup together, plus the orange bitters (if using). If you don't have a cocktail shaker, shake them in a clean glass screwtop jar.
3. Add some ice cubes to the glass and pour in the margarita mixture, taking care not to splash it onto the salty rim. Add one drop of liquid smoke to impart a smoky flavour (optional) and enjoy.

Variations
- For a really smoky flavour, use some smoked sea salt.
- Give this some heat by adding a little chilli powder to the sea salt before dipping the glass.
- For a warming alcoholic version, make up some cocoa according to the instructions on the packet and add 2–3 tablespoons mezcal and a sugar cube to each mug. Stir well and top with some toasted marshmallows.

CAMPFIRE HOT TODDIES

SERVES 2 | PREP 5 MINUTES

2 tea bags (black, not green, tea)
4 tsp lemon juice
2 tbsp runny honey
90ml (3fl oz/6 tbsp) whisky or bourbon

Tip: Smoky flavoured teas, like lapsang souchong, are particularly good for campfire toddies.

If it's a cold evening and you need to warm up, these hot toddies are just the thing. And you don't need ice cubes, sugar syrup, cocktail shakers and all the usual paraphernalia – just some tea bags, honey, fresh or bottled lemon juice and a bottle of whiskey or bourbon, of course.

1. Put a tea bag in each mug and bring some water to the boil over the campfire or camping stove. Pour the boiling water over the tea bags so the mugs are half to two-thirds full. Leave to steep for 3 minutes.
2. Remove the tea bags and add 2 teaspoons lemon juice and 1 tablespoon honey to each mug. Stir well until the honey dissolves.
3. Stir in the whisky and drink while piping hot or warm.

Variations
• If you don't like tea, omit the tea bag and just add boiling water to the whisky, lemon juice and honey.
• Use Indian chai tea, add a twist of lemon or orange zest and stir with a cinnamon stick.
• Use dark rum instead of whisky.
• Use maple syrup instead of honey.

SPICY MARSHMALLOW HOT CHOCOLATE

SERVES 2 | PREP 5 MINUTES | COOK 5 MINUTES

2 tbsp cocoa powder

350ml (12fl oz/1½ cups) milk
   (dairy or dairy-free)

brown sugar, to taste

½ tsp ground cinnamon

a pinch of ground nutmeg

a pinch of cayenne

marshmallows, for toasting

Everybody loves this warming campfire hot chocolate, especially children. It's so easy to make and a very calming and relaxing drink to get you in the mood for bed and a good night's sleep. The milk contains sleep-friendly tryptophan and vitamin D, and the cocoa is a good source of magnesium, which helps you unwind and relaxes aching muscles.

1. Put a tablespoon of cocoa powder in each mug. Heat the milk in a pan over the campfire or on a camping stove. Just before it boils, pour it onto the cocoa and mix well.
2. Stir in sugar to sweeten, together with the ground spices.
3. Toast some marshmallows on a toasting fork or skewer over the fire (see page 53) or in a gas flame on the stove.
4. Pile the marshmallows on top of the spicy cocoa and enjoy.

Variations
- Use drinking chocolate instead of cocoa.
- Add some strong instant coffee powder to the cocoa.
- Top with some whipped cream (use an aerosol can).
- Add some ground cardamom, vanilla seeds or extract.

INDEX

Shot on location at Campwell Campsite, Bath
https://campwell.co.uk

Applewood logs and charcoal supplied by Woodsmith Wood Ltd.
https://woodsmithwood.com

Additional props, campfire tripods, coolers supplied by Nomad Supply Store
https://nomadsupplystore.com